TRON THEATRE

Black Hole Sign

By Uma Nada-Rajah

Cast

Helen Logan	Crea
Dani Heron	Ani / Apparition Mary
Betty Valencia	Lina / Isla / Apparition Gloria
Martin Docherty	Billy / Mr Turnbull / Mr Ivan Hopper
Beruce Khan	Mr Iain Hopper
Ann Louise Ross	Tersia / NMC Panel Chair

Creative Team

Uma Nada-Rajah	Playwright
Gareth Nicholls	Director
Anna Orton	Set & Costume Design
Michael John McCarthy	Composer & Sound Design
Lizzie Powell	Lighting Designer
Emily Jane Boyle	Movement Director

Production Team

Kevin McCallum	Production Manager
Renny Robertson	Head of Lighting & Sound
Dave Bailey	Lighting & Sound
Alasdair Hood	Lighting & Sound
Laura Skinner	Production Manager
Alex Hatfield	Technical Manager
Suzanne Goldberg	Stage Manager
Fi Elliott	Venue Technician
Adi Currie	Venue Technician
Ruth Burgon	Deputy Stage Manager
Babette Wickham-Riddick	Assistant Stage Manager (Stage Manager, Edinburgh)
Jennie Lööf	Costume Supervisor
Beth Allnutt	Wardrobe Assistant

Uma Nada-Rajah is a playwright based in Kilbarchan, Scotland. She was one of the BBC's Scottish Voices 2020 and was the Starter Female Political Comedy writer-in-residence at the National Theatre of Scotland.

Uma is a graduate of École Philippe Gaulier and a previous participant of the Royal Court's Young Writers' Programme and the Traverse Theatre's Young Writers' Programme. In 2014 Uma won the New Playwrights Award from Playwrights' Studio Scotland. Her play *EXODUS* had its premiere at the Traverse Theatre in August 2022.

Awards include: Kavya Prize 2022, Shakespeare is Dead International Selection 2024.

She works as a staff nurse in critical care with NHS Scotland.

Gareth Nicholls is Artistic Director of the Traverse Theatre. For the Traverse, his shows include *So Young* by Douglas Maxwell, *The Grand Old Opera House Hotel* by Isobel McArthur, *Wilf* by James Ley, *Still* by Frances Poet, *The Monstrous Heart* by Oliver Emanuel, *Crocodile Fever* by Meghan Tyler, *Ulster American* by David Ireland, *Arctic Oil* by Clare Duffy, *How To Disappear* by Morna Pearson and *Letters to Morrissey* by Gary McNair.

Other productions include: *Kidnapped* by Isobel McArthur (National Theatre of Scotland), *Trainspotting* by Irvine Welsh, *Blackbird* by David Harrower, *Into That Darkness* by Gitta Sereny, *Vanya* by Sam Holcroft (Citizens Theatre); *God Of Carnage* by Yasmina Reza, *Under Milk Wood* by Dylan Thomas (Tron Theatre), *A Gamblers Guide To Dying* by Gary McNair (Show & Tell), *Educating Ronnie* by Joe Douglas (Utter).

His work has toured extensively across the UK as well as transferring to Australia, New Zealand, Ireland and USA. Gareth has won numerous awards including six Scotsman Fringe Firsts.

Previously, he was Main-Stage Director in Residence at the Citizens Theatre, Artist In Residence at Imaginate International Children's Festival and an Emerging Artist at the National Theatre of Scotland.

Anna Orton is a designer working across Theatre, Dance, Opera and Exhibition. Her previous work exhibiting, performing and curating as a visual artist in some of Scotland's most pioneering spaces continues to influence her work in performance design.

Her design work includes the multi-award-winning production of Handel's *Messiah* directed by Tom Morris, which premiered at *Bristol Old Vic* and was followed by a national cinema and online streaming release. Previous work for Tron Theatre includes Carole Churchill's *Escaped Alone* directed by Joanna Bowman.

Recent credits include: *Oedipus Rex, The Tsar Has His Photo Taken* and *La Bohème* (Scottish Opera), *GUNTER* (Dirty Hare/ Royal Court), *VL* (Francesca Moody Productions/Roundabout), *LEAR* (Raw Material), *Blond Eckbert* and *Acis & Galatea* (Hans Otto Theatre, Germany), *Adults* (Traverse Theatre), *Kidnapped* (National Theatre of Scotland), *This Is Memorial Device* (Royal Lyceum Theatre Edinburgh, Fringe First Award/ UK Tour), *Robin Hood Legend of the Forgotten Forest* and *King Lear (*Bristol Old Vic), *Peter Pan and Wendy* and *A Christmas Carol* (Pitlochry- Shortlisted for *Best Emerging Designer*, World Stage Design Awards 2021), *Welcome Home* (Soho Theatre) and *The Effect* (English Theatre Frankfurt).

She has designed for many prestigious companies including *Live Theatre Newcastle, English Touring Opera, Buxton Opera Festival, Theatre Ad Infinitum, Bath Theatre Royal, Stellar Quines, The New Theatre Dublin* and *The Watermill Theatre* amongst others.

She was recipient of the *OLD VIC 12 Designer Affiliation* in 2019, an MGC Futures recipient in 2021 and was the first JMK runner up in 2023. Anna's designs have also been nominated for the Offies and CATS Awards. She has MA in Theatre Design from Bristol Old Vic Theatre School and an MA in Fine art from Duncan of Jordanstone Collage of Art and Design.

Michael John McCarthy is a composer, sound designer and theatre-maker, originally from West Cork, currently based in Glasgow. He has worked on over ninety theatre productions, including twelve Scotsman Edinburgh Fringe First Award winners. Theatre includes: *Pride & Prejudice*(*sort of)* (Tron Theatre/Criterion Theatre/Touring); *The Duchess (of Malfi)* (Trafalgar Theatre/Lyceum Edinburgh); *Two Sisters* (Lyceum Edinburgh); *The Fair Maid of the West* (Royal Shakespeare Company); *England and Son* (Roundabout/HOME Manchester); *The Grand Opera House Hotel* (Traverse Theatre/Dundee Rep); *What Girls Are Made Of* (Raw Material); *Kidnapped* (National Theatre of Scotland); *Little Red Riding Hood* (Citizens Theatre); *Cinderella* (Dundee Rep); *The Last Return* (Druid Theatre Company); *The Strange Undoing of Prudencia Hart* (Royal Exchange Manchester); *NORA: A Doll's House* (Young Vic/Citizens Theatre); *Jimmy's Hall* (Abbey Theatre); *The Hour We Knew Nothing of Each Other*, *Glory On Earth*, *A Number*, *The Weir* and *Bondagers* (Royal Lyceum Theatre Edinburgh); *I Can Go Anywhere*, *Crocodile Fever*, *Ulster American* and *How To Disappear* (Traverse Theatre); *Tay Bridge*, *August: Osage County*, *The Cheviot, The Stag & The Black, Black Oil* and *The BFG* (Dundee Rep); *Trainspotting*, *Into That Darkness* and *Fever Dream: Southside* (Citizens Theatre); and *Rocket Post*, *In Time O' Strife*, *The Day I Swapped My Dad for Two Goldfish* and *Dolls* (National Theatre of Scotland).

Work for screen includes the documentaries *Where You're Meant To Be* and *Pitching Up*.

His band Album Club released their debut LP in May 2022. It reached #6 in the UK Vinyl Albums chart, and #2 in the Scottish Albums chart, spending six weeks in the Top 100.

Lizzie Powell is a Lighting Designer working internationally in theatre and opera. Her credits in theatre include: *The Fifth Step*, *Thrown*, *Orphans*, *Red Dust Road*, *Adam*, *Knives in Hens*, *Venus As A Boy* (National Theatre of Scotland); *A View from the Bridge* (Tron Theatre); *The Events* (Cumbernauld Theatre); *There's a Place* (Perth Theatre); *Robin Red Breast* (Factory International Manchester); The Outrun (Edinburgh Lyceum); *Macbeth – An Undoing* (Edinburgh Lyceum Theatre/Rose Theatre/Kingston Theatre for a New Audience/New York); *August: Osage County* (Malmo Stadsteater); *Same Team: A Street Soccer Story*, *The Grand Opera House Hotel* (Traverse Theatre); *Cat on a Hot Tin Roof*, *The Mountaintop*, *Mother Courage*, *Anna Karenina*, *The Mighty Walzer* (Royal Exchange); *Comedy of Errors*, *Endgame*, *The Libertine* (Citizens Theatre); *James IV, What Girls are Made Of*, (Raw Material); *King John*, *Macbeth* (Royal Shakespeare Company); *Avalanche: A Love Story* (Barbican/Sydney Theatre Company); *The Da Vinci Code*, *Dial M for Murder* (Simon Friend Productions); *Our Ladies of Perpetual Succour* (West End/National Theatre of Scotland); *Victory Condition*, *B*, *Human Animals*, *Violence and Son* (Royal Court Theatre); *Our Town* (Regent's Park Open Air Theatre); *Romeo & Juliet* (Crucible Theatre, Sheffield); and *Cyrano De Bergerac* (Citizens Theatre/National Theatre of Scotland/Royal Lyceum Theatre Edinburgh).

Emily Jane Boyle is a highly acclaimed movement director whose theatre work spans major stages across the UK and internationally. Her credits include *Leopoldstadt* (West End/Broadway), *Pride and Prejudice (sort of)* (West End/Tron), *Make It Happen* and *Kidnapped* (National Theatre of Scotland), *Hedda Gabler* and *Jumpy* (Lyceum), *The Grand Old Opera House Hotel*, *Adults*, and *WILF* (Traverse), and *Exit the King* (National Theatre). She has also worked on *Oresteia: This Restless House*, *Trainspotting*, *Cuttin' a Rug*, and *Lanark* (Citizens Theatre); *The Mirror and the Light*, *The Fair Maid of the West*, and *Henry VI* (RSC); and numerous productions at Dundee Rep, the Young Vic, Leeds Playhouse, Shakespeare's Globe, Regent's Park Open Air Theatre, and internationally with Goodspeed and Faena. Screen work includes *Summerwater* (Channel 4), *The Crown* (Netflix), *Our Ladies* (Sony), *Plain Sight* (ITV), *God Help the Girl* (Sundance), *Still Game: Live*, *Two Doors Down*, and the *Glasgow Commonwealth Games* (BBC).

Helen Logan's *(Crea)* extensive stage work includes *To Save the Sea* (Sleeping Warrior), *Lena* (Feather Productions /Assembly/Tour), *Local Hero* (Royal Lyceum), *Hamlet* (Bard in the Botanics), and multiple seasons at Pitlochry Festival Theatre, with credits ranging from *Chicago* and *My Fair Lady* to *Amadeus*. She has also performed with Perth Theatre, A Play, A Pie and A Pint, and on national tours. Screen credits include *Lockerbie: A Search For Truth* (Sky), *River City* (BBC), and *The Descent* (Celador/Pathé).

Dani Heron's (*Ani / Apparition Mary)* stage work includes *Underwood Lane*, *Alright Sunshine* and *Radiant Vermin* (Tron Theatre), *Adults* and *90 Days* (Traverse Theatre), *Tally's Blood* (Perth Theatre & tour), and *Peter Gynt* (National Theatre/EFT). She has also appeared with A Play, A Pie & A Pint, National Theatre of Scotland, Royal Lyceum, and in the West End. TV credits include *Crime* (Britbox), *Murder Island* (Channel 4), and *Casualty* (BBC).

Betty Valencia *(Lina / Isla / Apparition Gloria)* trained at New College Lanarkshire. Theatre work includes *Ivor* (A Play, a Pie & A Pint); *Aladdin, Rapunzel: A Hair Braiding Adventure* (Macrobert Arts Centre); *Disfunction* (A Play, A Pie & A Pint); *Local Hero* (Chichester Festival Theatre); *Orphans* (National Theatre of Scotland); *Cinderella* (Perth Theatre); *We Came To Dance* (Yardheads); *This Girl Laughs This Girl Cries This Girl Does Nothing* (Stellar Quines/Imaginate); *August: Osage County* (Dundee Rep Theatre). Film work includes *The Last Bus*.

Martin Docherty (*Billy / Mr Turnbull / Mr Ivan Hopper*) is an actor and writer with an extensive career across stage and screen. His theatre work includes *Moorcroft*, *Risk*, *Club Asylum*, *Antigone* and *Cooking With Elvis* (Tron Theatre); *Venice Preserved*, *Snow White*, *Anville*, *Scarfed for Life* and *Whatever Happened to the Jaggy Nettles* (Citizens Theatre); *Decky Does a Bronco* (Grid Iron); *The Hard Man* (Finborough); *Stitchers* (Jermyn Street); *Thieves and Boy* (A Play, A Pie and A Pint); *The Invisible Hand* (Edinburgh Fringe); *The Year of the Hare* (Rymateatteri); and *Continuous Growth* (Helsinki Group). He also co-wrote and performed the one-man show *Mcluckie's Line* with Martin Travers. On television, he has appeared in *River City*, *The Chief*, *Gary Tank Commander* and *Rab C. Nesbitt* (BBC Scotland); *Still Game* and *Dear Green Place* (Effingee); *Outlander* (Sony/Starz); *Father Brown*, *Young James Herriot* and *Case Histories* (BBC); and *Annika* (Black Camel). He was the subject of *Marty Goes to Hollywood*, which won a New Talent Scottish BAFTA Award in 2015. His film credits include *Cloud Atlas* (Warner Bros), *Borges and Me* (Big Beach), and *Wild Rose* (Fable Pictures/Film4).

Beruce Khan's *(Mr Iain Hopper)* screen work includes the feature film *Greenland: Migration* and TV credits such as *The Capture* (Season 3), *Vera*, *Britannia*, *War of the Worlds* (Canal+), *Canoe* (ITV), and *The Chief* (BBC1 Scotland). His extensive theatre career includes productions at leading venues such as the RSC (*A Christmas Carol*, *Twelfth Night*), Shakespeare's Globe (*Hamlet* world tour, *The Winter's Tale*, *Hansel and Gretel*), Regent's Park

Open Air Theatre (*Henry V*, *As You Like It*), Southwark Playhouse (*Yellowfin*), Donmar (*Adult Children*), Hampstead Theatre (*Ravens*), Chichester Festival Theatre (*Shadowlands*), and the National Theatre and West End. He also appeared in *We Are The Best* (Live Theatre) and *Neville's Island* (Queen's Theatre).

Ann Louise Ross *(Tersia / NMC Panel Chair)* is a multi-award-winning stage and screen actor with a career spanning decades and a long-standing member of the Dundee Rep Ensemble. Her extensive theatre credits include *Make It Happen* (National Theatre of Scotland/Dundee Rep); *Doubt* (Dundee Rep); *Cyprus Avenue* (Tron Theatre); *The Grand Old Opera House Hotel* (Traverse/Dundee Rep); *Peter Gynt* (National Theatre/EIF); *The Dark Carnival* (Vanishing Point/Citizens Theatre/Dundee Rep); *Doctor Faustus* (Citizens/West Yorkshire Playhouse); *The Guid Sisters* (NTS/Royal Lyceum); and *Mary Queen of Scots Got Her Head Chopped Off* and *Age of Arousal* (Royal Lyceum). As a key member of Dundee Rep Ensemble for over 25 years, she has earned wide acclaim for roles in *Gypsy (Rose)*, *Sweeney Todd* (Mrs Lovett), and *The Winter's Tale* (Paulina). Her stage work has earned her a CATS Award for Best Female Performance (*Further Than the Furthest Thing*), a TMA Award for Best Supporting Performance in a Musical (*Sunshine on Leith*), and a CATS Award for Best Supporting Actress (*The Winter's Tale*). On screen, Ann Louise has appeared in *Good Omens 2, Shetland, The Farm, Case Histories, Rebus, Bob Servant Independent, Trainspotting, The Acid House* Trilogy, *Whisky Galore, River City, Stone of Destiny, The Witch's Daughter, The Key, The Bill, Life Support, Looking After Jo Jo,* and *Hamish Macbeth*. She is also beloved for her role as Grannie Island in CBeebies' *Katie Morag* series.

Black Hole Sign was commissioned by the **Traverse Theatre**. Co-produced by the **Tron Theatre Company** & **Traverse Theatre** in association with the **National Theatre of Scotland**.

This edition was published to coincide with the first run of Black Hole Sign at Glasgow's Tron Theatre 19th September – 4th October 2025 and at Edinburgh's Traverse Theatre 8th-18th October 2025.

The Traverse is a champion of performance, experience and discovery. Enabling people to access and engage with theatre is our fundamental mission, and we want our work to represent, speak to and be seen by the broadest cross-section of society. Across our programme, you can encounter trailblazing creativity that offers unique opportunities to explore the world around us, connect with the lives of others and spark that vital curiosity in what it is to be human.

Reflecting on our successes these past six decades, as we make our way past our milestone 60th year despite this precarious cultural sector, we see a present opportunity to redefine and broaden routes into artistic creation and expression. Our programming model holds space for community-inspired and co-created collaborative work. Alongside traditional plays and commissioning trajectories, these works with social change at its core make for a resonant, relevant, and impactful programme. We make theatre and tell stories with heart, for audiences across the UK and internationally, always aiming to reach those who may not traditionally visit the theatre or connect with live performances. As Scotland's premier new work theatre, this commitment drives each strand of our work, ensuring that the Traverse continues for another six decades and long into the future.

Our year-round programme bursts with new stories, live and digital performances that challenge, inform and entertain our audiences. We empower artists and audiences to make sense of the world today, providing a safe space to question, learn, empathise and – crucially – encounter different people and experiences. Conversation and the coming together of groups are central to a democratic society, and we support equal expression and understanding for the future of a healthy national and international community.

Here's to the Traverse and all who have created with, played for, visited, and continue to champion everything we are. Our past successes drive our present and future direction, in the knowledge that our unique ability to nurture new talent and engage audiences through ambitious storytelling has never been more crucial in creating and sustaining a vibrant theatre landscape that reflects and challenges the world today.

Find out more about our work: traverse.co.uk

TRON THEATRE

Established in 1982, Tron Theatre has built a renowned reputation for producing and presenting ambitious, contemporary, and proudly subversive theatre, reflecting the world we live in and representing the people of Glasgow and Scotland. It has established itself as a vital, creative hub for the Scottish theatre sector and as a powerhouse of home-grown, new and contemporary Scottish work.

The Tron building, with its centuries-old heritage, stands proudly on the edge of the city, where the city centre meets the ever-changing East End of Glasgow. As well as the Tron's self-produced programme, it is a critical cog in the UK's touring infrastructure, a vital incubator and supporter of emerging and mid-career talent, as well as facilitating vibrant participatory arts opportunities for people across the city.

Recent Tron Theatre Company productions include *Man's Best Friend* by Douglas Maxwell, *A View from the Bridge* by Arthur Miller, *Radiant Vermin* by Philip Ridley, *Escaped Alone* by Caryl Churchill, Gary McNair's *Nae Expectations*, David Ireland's *Cyprus Avenue*, Eilidh Loan's *Moorcroft*, and Isobel McArthur's *Pride and Prejudice* (*sort of)* which had its premiere at the venue in 2018, toured nationally, and opened in the autumn of 2021 at the Criterion Theatre in London's West End, receiving an Olivier Award in 2022 for Best Entertainment or Comedy.

www.tron.co.uk

National Theatre of Scotland is a Theatre Without Walls. We don't have our own venue, instead, we're able to bring theatre to you wherever you are. From the biggest stages to the smallest community halls, we showcase Scottish culture at home and around the world. We have performed in airports and tower blocks, submarines and swimming pools, telling stories in ways you have never seen before.

We want to bring the joy of theatre to everyone. Since we were founded in 2006, we have produced hundreds of shows and toured all over the world. We strive to amplify the voices that need to be heard, tell the stories that need to be told and take work to wherever audiences are to be found.

To find out about the full team at National Theatre of Scotland please visit:

nationaltheatrescotland.com/about/our-people or follow us on social media @ntsonline

National Theatre of Scotland is Core funded by

Traverse Theatre Funders

The Traverse extends grateful thanks to all of its supporters, including those who prefer to remain anonymous. Their valuable contributions ensure that the Traverse continues to champion stories and storytellers in all forms, help develop the next generation of creative talent and lead vital projects in our local community, Scotland and beyond.

With your help, we can write the next scene of our story. Visit traverse.co.uk/support-us to find out more.

Traverse Theatre (Scotland) is a Limited Company (SC076037) and a Scottish Charity (SC002368) with its Registered Office at 10 Cambridge Street, Edinburgh, Scotland, EH1 2ED.

Individual Supporters

Premier
Angus McLeod
David Rodgers

Diamond
Alan & Penny Barr
Kirsten Lamb

Platinum
Iain Millar
Mike & Carol Ramsay

Gold
Carola Bronte-Stewart
Michael Minieka
Neil & Stephanie

Silver
Judy & Steve
Bridget Stevens
Allan Wilson
Gill McDonald
Chris & Susan Gifford
Lesley Preston
Joan Aitken
John Healy
Lucy Caird
Richard Finlay
Susan Tritton
Leslie Hurst

Bronze
Katie Bradford
John Richards
Heather Alderson
Jenny Halpin
Barbara Braham

Sadie McKinlay
Vivienne Phillips
Jon Best
Patricia Pugh
Keith Thomson
Lewis Derrick
David McCrone

Trusts, Foundations & Grants

The Backstage Trust
Dr David Summers Charitable Trust
Enterprise Arts Trust
Foundation Scotland
The Foyle Foundation
Gordon Fraser Charitable Trust
John Thaw Foundation
James Thom Howat Charitable Trust
Playwrights '73 Scheme

Grant funders

The Traverse Theatre is funded by Creative Scotland and The City of Edinburgh Council.

In Residence Partners

The Traverse Theatre has the support of the Playwrights '73 Awards Scheme (Previously Peggy Ramsay/Film 4). The Traverse Theatre is further supported by IASH, the Institute of Advanced Research in the Humanities, the University of Edinburgh.

Hospitality Partners

DINE Edinburgh
Edinburgh Beer Factory
Secret Garden Gin Distillery
Hey Girls
Vegware

ALBA | CHRUTHACHAIL

Traverse Theatre

David Bailey	Lighting & Sound Technician
Siobhan Clark	Senior Producer
Linda Crooks	Executive Producer & Chief Executive
Caitlin Cumberland	Head of Communications
David Drummond	General Manager
Ellen Gledhill	Executive Director
Ottilie Hill Smith	Development Officer
Alasdair Hood	Lighting & Sound Technician
Becca King	Class Act Coordinator & Productions Assistant
Kevin McCallum	Head of Production
Anne McCluskey	Senior Creative Producer
Aude Naudi-Bonnemaison	Artistic Administrator
Gareth Nicholls	Artistic Director
Rachel O'Regan	Marketing Associate
Julie Pigott	Director of Finance & Operations
Pauleen Rafferty	Payroll & HR Manager
Georgia-Lee Roberts	Customer Experience Manager
Renny Robertson	Head of Lighting & Sound
Serden Salih	Digital Content Associate
Lauren Scott	Senior Communications Officer
Staci Shaw	Sales & Welcome Team Member
Gordon Strachan	Ticketing & Data Manager
Alice Underwood	Finance & Administration Officer

Also working for the Traverse

Courtney Bassett, Debbie Bentley, Stacey Brown, Eve Buglass, Rachel Clinton, Stephen Cox, Katie Edmundson, Laura Gentile, Jazmin Gilham, Katie Gregory, Devon Holloway, Lesley Howard, Jack Hunter Nicholson, Darren Hunsley, Sophia Irvine-Fortescue, Amandine Jalon, Sam Johnston, Lottie Lewis-Morton, Eli Lozinski, Madeleine MacGregor, Mollie MacGregor, Zoe Maunder, Alison McFarlane, Abbie Meldrum, Tiger Mitchell, Afton Moran, Ellie Moran, Chris Mundy, Rory Murray, Karolina Oleskiewicz, Nara Schneider, Coco Schogler, Rob Small, Heidi Steel, Maya Thomas, Eve Thomson, Aria Tsvetanova, Huw Turnbull, Isaac Vincent, Jessica Wain.

Writers in Residence

Ciara Elizabeth Smyth
Michael John O'Neill

Associate Artists

Bryony Shanahan
Adrian Hon
Emma Dorfman

Traverse Theatre Board of Directors

Helen Forsyth (Chair)
Morag Ballantyne
Kate Gibb
Kieran Hurley

Zakia Moulaoui Guery
Dave Moutrey
Rebecca O'Brien
May Sumbwanyambe

Tron Theatre Funders

THE TRON GRATEFULLY ACKNOWLEDGES SUPPORT FROM

Creative Scotland

CORPORATE PARTNERS

G.H. Digital Print

TRUSTS AND FOUNDATIONS

Bellahouston Bequest Fund, Birkdale Trust, Boshier Hinton Foundation, Calton Area Partnership Fund, WA Cargill Fund, Cruden Foundation, The Endrick Trust, Esmee Fairbairn TASK Fund, Hugh Fraser Foundation, Gannochy Trust, Garfield Weston Foundation, Glasgow City Council Green Grant, Glasgow City Council Minor Improvements Grant, Glasgow City Heritage Trust, Dr. Guthrie's Association, Kilpatrick Fraser Charitable Trust, WM Mann Foundation, John Mather Trust, Nairn Family Trust, Rab Noakes Bequest, The Wolfson Foundation.

TRON CHAMPIONS

Julie Austin, Lorna Baird, Kati Byrne, Peter Lawson, David Lightbody, Fiona McDonald, Rita Rae, Andy & Sandra West

PATRONS 2024-25

Thomas Collins, Stewart & Frankie Coulter, Ruth Crawford, Monica Deans, Angela Donoghue, Mike Glancy, Susan Hunt, Eleanor Hyland, Andrew Lockyer, Stewart MacKay, Susan McBride, Frank & Kathleen McGoldrick, Tony McGoldrick, Helen McLaren, Alison Mitchell, Helen Morton, Kenneth Murray, Noelle O'Rourke, Fraser Reid, Sylvia Rossi, Fred & Irene Shedden, Craig & Paula Stark, Mandy Stewart.

Special thanks to Helen Jean Miller, a long-time Tron Theatre supporter, who generously left us a gift in her will for our work

SUPPORTING THE TRON THEATRE

More than ever before we need your contributions to support the work of our creative community, offer opportunities to young people and deliver outreach work in our immediate locale and across the city. You support our work every time you visit the Tron Theatre.

For more information on how you can support the Tron Theatre visit
tron.co.uk/supporting_the_tron_theatre or email: **development@tron.co.uk**

ALBA | CHRUTHACHAIL

TRON THEATRE

Artistic Director	Jemima Levick
Interim Executive Director	Neil Murray
Artistic Producer	Viviane Hullin
Artistic Producer (maternity cover)	Laura Clark
Assistant Producer	Cait Irvine
Creative Learning Manager	Lisa Keenan
Creative Learning Coordinator	Catherine Ward-Stoddart
Production Manager	Laura Skinner
Technical Manager	Alex Hatfield
Stage Manager	Suzanne Goldberg
Venue Technician	Fi Elliott
Venue Technician	Adi Currie
Head of Marketing & Communications	Lindsay Mitchell
Marketing & Communications Officer	Danielle Redmond Gray
Building Manager	Iain MacLeod
Head of Venue Management	Khaliq Ahmed
Duty Managers	Hazel Ann Crawford, Rosie Dahlstrom, Emma Gilluley, Michelle Lynch, Finlay McGarry
Administration Assistant	Rosie Hall

Thanks to all our box office, front of house, café/bar assistants and the cleaning team.

Board of Directors
Roberta Doyle (Chair), Julie Chambers, Katie Douglas, Robert Softley Gale, Sunita Hinduja, Gillian McCormack, Johnny McKnight, Ross Nicol, Geoff Nolan and Nicola Walls.

Tron Theatre Company is a supported by Creative Scotland, is a company limited by guarantee (SC077475) and a Scottish Registered Charity No: SC012081.

Black Hole Sign

Uma Nada-Rajah was a member of the Young Writers' Programme at the Traverse Theatre and is a graduate of École Philippe Gaulier. She is a recipient of the New Playwrights Award and the winner of the Inaugural Kavya Prize. Uma is currently under commission to the Almeida Theatre in London and the Citizens Theatre in Glasgow. She also works as a nurse for NHS Scotland. Theatre credits include *The Great Replacement* (A Play, a Pie and a Pint, Òran Mór), *Exodus* (Traverse Theatre), *Toy Plastic Chicken* (A Play, a Pie and a Pint, Òran Mór and Traverse Theatre; BBC iPlayer), *The Domestic* and *Rapunzel* (National Theatre of Scotland).

by the same author from Faber

EXODUS

UMA NADA-RAJAH

Black Hole Sign

faber

First published in 2025
by Faber and Faber Limited
The Bindery, 51 Hatton Garden
London, EC1N 8HN

Typeset by Brighton Gray
Printed and bound in the UK by CPI Group (Ltd), Croydon CR0 4YY

All rights reserved
© Uma Nada-Rajah, 2025

Uma Nada-Rajah is hereby identified as author
of this work in accordance with Section 77 of the
Copyright, Designs and Patents Act 1988

All rights whatsoever in this work, amateur or professional,
are strictly reserved. Applications for permission for any use
whatsoever including performance rights must be made in
advance, prior to any such proposed use, to
United Agents, 12–26 Lexington Street, London W1F OLE

No performance may be given unless a licence
has first been obtained

This book is sold subject to the condition that it shall not,
by way of trade or otherwise, be lent, resold, hired out
or otherwise circulated without the publisher's prior consent
in any form of binding or cover other than that in which
it is published and without a similar condition including
this condition being imposed on the subsequent purchaser

A CIP record for this book
is available from the British Library

ISBN 978–0–571–40216–8

Printed and bound in the UK on FSC® certified paper in line with our continuing
commitment to ethical business practices, sustainability and the environment.

For further information see faber.co.uk/environmental-policy

Our authorised representative in the EU for product safety is
Easy Access System Europe, Mustamäe tee 50, 10621 Tallinn, Estonia
gpsr.requests@easproject.com

2 4 6 8 10 9 7 5 3 1

Black Hole Sign was first performed at the Tron Theatre, Glasgow, on 19 September 2025, and at the Traverse Theatre, Edinburgh, on 8 October 2025. The cast was as follows:

Crea Helen Logan
Ani / 'Mary' Dani Heron
Lina / Isla / 'Gloria' Betty Valencia
Billy / Mr Turnbull / Mr Ivan Hopper Martin Docherty
Mr Iain Hopper Beruce Khan
Tersia / NMC Panel Chair Ann Louise Ross

Director Gareth Nicholls
Set & Costume Designer Anna Orton
Composer & Sound Designer Michael John McCarthy
Lighting Designer Lizzie Powell
Movement Director Emily Jane Boyle

Black Hole Sign was commissioned by the Traverse Theatre and co-produced by the Tron Theatre Company and Traverse Theatre in association with the National Theatre of Scotland.

This play is dedicated to all nurses,
especially my auntie Susheela

Acknowledgements

I am indebted to the nurses I have interviewed in the process of writing this play, and to all the actors and nurses who contributed invaluable feedback during the development process. I would first like to extend my gratitude to Gareth Nicholls, Jemima Levick, Giles Smart, and Martin Robinson. Also: Tom Alexander, Ella Appleton, Maureen Boyd, Lee Byrne, Daniel Donnelly, Matt Green, Mazz Hamidi, Debbie Hannan, Rose Hilton, Ese Ighorae, Rosie Kellagher, Paul Laverty, Emily Ling-Williams, Eilidh Loan, Jane MacDonald, Jack MacGregor, Anna Russell Martin, Jim Martin, Jonathan Mesh, Anne McCluskey, Michael John McCarthy, Johnny McKnight, Lynn Nottage, Adura Onashile, Michael John O'Neill, Anna Orton, Silas Parry, Gabe Quigley, Shibani Sathiananthan, Louise Stevens, Joanne Thompson, and Jonathan Watson. To all the hospital staff I currently and have previously worked with, as well as the Tron Theatre, the Traverse Theatre, Faber & Faber, the National Theatre of Scotland, the Scottish Society of Playwrights and Playwrights' Studio Scotland.

The Sibyl with frenzied mouth uttering things not to be laughed at, unadorned and unperfumed, yet reaches to a thousand years with her voice by the aid of God.

Heraclitus

Antigone is right, but Creon is not wrong.

Albert Camus

Characters

STAFF

Crea
Senior Charge Nurse (SCN), fifties

Ani
staff nurse, thirties

Lina
student nurse, early twenties

Billy
porter, early sixties

PATIENTS

Mr Iain Hopper
intracerebral haemorrhage (palliative), forties

Tersia
delirium secondary to UTI, late seventies

Isla
extensive bruising and knee and elbow fractures from reported fall, late teens

Turnbull
foreign object to gluteus maximus, early sixties

OTHER PARTS

**Mr Ivan Hopper, NMC Panel Chair,
'Mary', 'Sindhu', 'Young Crea'**

Doubling

The configuration below works for an ensemble of six actors:

> The actor playing the role of Lina
> may also play Isla and 'Sindhu'.
>
> The actor playing the role of Ani
> may also play 'Mary'.
>
> The actor playing Billy
> may also play Turnbull and Mr Ivan Hopper.
>
> The actor playing Tersia
> may also play NMC Panel Chair.

Time and Place

Black Hole Sign is set across three generations of nurses over one winter's nightshift.

Pod B is one of four 'major' bases in the A&E or Acute Medical Receiving Unit of a busy regional NHS hospital. There is limited flow through the unit due to bed-waits, and Pod B is predominantly being managed by nursing staff.

Two narratives move forward in linear time. The main action of the play is composed of the events of the nightshift of the 21st of December. The secondary action, taking place one year later, is a Nursing and Midwifery Council (NMC) Hearing, concerning the Fitness to Practice of Senior Charge Nurse Crea.

BLACK HOLE SIGN

Notes

Casting should reflect the diversity of the NHS
as an institution.

In the original production, Apparition 'Sindhu' was
renamed 'Gloria' to reflect the actor's background.

The 'HOLE' of the collapsed roof is real; however, it is seen
by the audience from Mr Hopper's perspective. Through his
deterioration it becomes all-encompassing. This starts as a
leak in Act One. It is a full-sized HOLE by the time Hopper
loses consciousness in Act Two. By the death at the end of
Act Three, there is perhaps no ceiling, just night sky.
(See Martha Rosler, 'Cosmic Kitchen II' from the series
House Beautiful: The Colonies, 1966–1972.)

A BILLOWING CURTAIN haunts Hopper. The motion of the
curtain is only sensed by the characters facing their own
mortality, though their reactions to it differ. Hopper feels
terror; Tersia views it sensuously; Isla is consumed by it.

There are four patients featured in the play. However, as
Nurse Ani states in handover, she is overseeing the care of
fourteen patients in Pod B, on top of her admissions in Act
Four. This should always feel clear to the audience, be it
through action or sound design.

Act One

1.1A

21st of December. Nightshift. Eight p.m.

Pod B is one of four 'major' bases in the A&E or Acute Medical Receiving Unit of a busy regional NHS hospital. The area consists of a few cubicles with disposable curtains, some plastic chairs and wheeled stretchers. There is also a linens cupboard, a drugs cupboard and a staff base with a swivel chair.

In the darkness, as the lights slowly come up, we see the figure of Isla, using her crutches to slowly cross the floor. She sings. Her voice is delicate and haunted. A draught ripples through the curtains as she passes.

As the lights begin to rise, we hear: Drip, drip, drip. There is a drip in the ceiling overhead.

Senior Charge Nurse (SCN) Crea enters. She is on her pre-nightshift walk around and is clutching a clipboard. She spots the drip in the ceiling. She dials a number on the handheld unit phone and walks off. We hear the unit phone:

Unit Phone Your call is important to us. You are number seventy-seven in the queue.

Lights come up on Staff Nurse Ani entering. She's nervous.

1.1B

Ani takes a deep breath and draws back a cubicle curtain.

Ani Mr Hopper?

Mr Ivan Hopper Yes?

Ani I'm afraid the news isn't good.

Mr Ivan Hopper It isn't?

Ani Would you like to sit down?

Mr Ivan Hopper sits. Stands. Sits.

I've brought you a glass of water. The doctor has been caught up. But she's asked if I could prepare you for what is to come.

Mr Ivan Hopper What do you mean? What is . . . to come?

Ani The doctor is on her way. She will discuss the results of your scan in more detail. She just wanted me to lay the groundwork.

Mr Ivan Hopper What exactly are you telling me?

Ani Um. I'm not qualified to –

Mr Ivan Hopper Just tell me what you know.

Ani (*hesitates*) They've seen something on your CT scan. A shadow.

Mr Ivan Hopper A shadow.

Ani Your scan shows an imaging marker called a Black Hole Sign. It's a bleed in your brain – a haemorrhage.

Mr Ivan Hopper A Black Hole?

Ani It predicts that the bleed is likely to expand. Spontaneously.

Mr Ivan Hopper Spontaneously?

Ani Yes.

Mr Ivan Hopper Just like that.

Ani Yes.

Mr Ivan Hopper How long do I have?

Ani She said it was difficult to tell. But. Given your symptoms.

Mr Ivan Hopper What does that mean?

Ani I'm not qualified to speculate. The doctor will be down any minute. She just wanted me to prepare you for the conversation to come. Is there anyone I can call for you in the meantime?

Mr Ivan Hopper There's the obvious person that you should call, but I've just realised I . . . I don't even like them.

Ani Well. Um. Is there anyone else?

Mr Ivan Hopper There are people that I love dearly. Yes. But I don't speak to them. The reasons for that suddenly seem petty.

Beat.

What scan?

Ani Oh I was referring to the CT scan you had an hour ago.

Mr Ivan Hopper I haven't had a scan since I broke my arm when I was a wee boy.

Ani Mr Hopper can you confirm your name and date of birth for me please?

Mr Ivan Hopper Ivan Hopper, 12th of July 1972. I came in here with –

Ani A tummy bug. Flip.

It's the wrong Mr Hopper.
Beat.

I'm afraid there's been a bit of a mix-up.
Entirely my fault.

Mr Ivan Hopper Wait. Am I not. Am I going to die?

Ani Not imminently. Not from a sore tummy.

Removes a box of tablets from her pocket.

If you follow the instruction on the label, your symptoms should clear up within a week.

Mr Ivan Hopper It's a lot to take in. I'm not going to – ?

Ani I'm sorry. I imagine you'll want to make a complaint. I'll get you the relevant paperwork.

Mr Ivan Hopper No. You don't understand.

Beat.

I think you've cured me.

Mr Ivan Hopper walks out – a new man.

Ani Wait! Don't forget your medication!!

Ani sighs. She reaches into her pocket and pulls out a can of energy drink. She necks it in one.

1.1C

Ani draws back the curtain to the next cubicle.
 Mr Iain Hopper stands in front of her.
 A spark of connection. The way that two strangers can instantly fall into rhythm.

Mr Hopper Hi.

Ani Hi.

Ani Are you Mr *Iain* Hopper?

Mr Hopper Yes.

Ani Can you confirm your name and date of birth for me please?

Mr Hopper Iain Hopper, 20th of December 1973.

Ani Would you like to sit down?

Mr Hopper I saw you downing that energy drink. You might need a seat more than I do.

Ani I'm all revved up. Raring to go.

She pauses. Motions to the chair.

Um. Please.

Mr Hopper sits down.
  The first gentle undulation of the BILLOWING CURTAIN.
Mr Hopper shudders.

Mr Hopper What's this about?

Ani Mr Hopper, I'm afraid the news isn't good.

1.2

Drip, drip, drip.
  The ceiling has worsened.
  Crea pulls a chair over and climbs on top of it to inspect the HOLE.
  Light shines down on Crea. A shift.

NMC PANEL HEARING: SECTION ONE

Nursing and Midwifery Council (NMC) Hearing. The linens cupboard transforms into a boardroom, from where the NMC Panel Chair speaks into a microphone. Crea remains in the world of the play while addressing the NMC Panel Chair.

NMC Panel Chair This is a Nursing and Midwifery Council Hearing with regards to your Fitness to Practice.

Crea I have been haunted by the events of the night of the 21st of December since their occurrence and have been waiting for this moment ever since.

NMC Panel Chair If you could confirm your name, role and registration number please.

Crea Crea Harrower. Senior Charge Nurse. Registration Number S05324X.

NMC Panel Chair The charge is Misconduct, leading to an untimely and avoidable death. Is that your understanding, Ms Harrower?

Crea Yes. It is.

NMC Panel Chair Let's begin.

Crea Wait. Before we start, I would like the panel to note that I assume sole responsibility for the untimely and avoidable death that occurred on that nightshift.

The events of that night cycle through my mind over and over again.

We fade back into the unit:
  Crea is on a chair inspecting the ceiling.
  She gently taps a bit of the surrounding area to assess its structural integrity.
  A small chunk of ceiling falls on her.

Bugger.

Billy, the head porter in his early sixties, enters. He's pushing Tersia in her wheelchair, returning her to A&E from the CT department.

Billy Crea!

At the sound of Billy's voice, Crea immediately dusts herself off.

Crea Billy. Hi.

Billy parks Tersia's wheelchair near to Crea.
  Tersia looks up and is struck by the HOLE *in the ceiling. She is acutely delirious because of a raging urinary tract infection (UTI) and has had a fall at home.*
  Tersia is older in age, glamorous and casually prophetic.

Tersia And so it begins.

Billy You've got a hole in your ceiling.

Crea I'm on hold with an external contractor. The out-of-hours service doesn't seem to function out-of-hours.

Crea checks the phone.

Unit Phone Your call is important to us. You are number seventy-six in the queue.

Billy (*looking up at the* HOLE) It's a shame it's been outsourced. The Estates Department would have fixed that for you on site.

Tersia (*to herself*) It all comes falling down.

Billy Oh. Um. This is Tersia. We've just come back from CT.

Crea Cheers, I can take her round from here, Billy.

Tersia (*to herself*) And then the endless darkness.

Crea Oh, it's nothing to worry about, Tersia. Just a wee draught. We'll get it sorted.

Tersia (Or so she thinks.)

Billy I didn't realise you were in tonight.

Crea I had a Band Six call in sick. I needed someone to fill the gap. Night five.

Billy Five nights in a row. You look –

Stops himself, aware of Crea's gaze.

You know you really wouldn't know it from looking at you.

Crea tucks a strand of hair behind her ear.

Tersia (*having caught this 'preening'*) Christ almighty.

Crea I've just done a risk assessment. There are currently ninety-six patients in the department. Closing this Pod will have a knock-on effect, likely causing more harm than keeping it open. Assuming the hole is . . . stable.

Crea scrutinises the HOLE.

What do you think . . . ?

Billy I'm a porter, Crea, not a bloody structural engineer.

Beat.

I'll get one of the boys to pop up on the roof and take a look.

Crea Cheers, Billy. That'd be a help.

Billy I like it.

Crea What?

Billy The hole. Not a single window in the entire emergency department. All these people born in here, die in here. Nice to be able to look up and see the stars.

Tersia Christ almighty. If yer gonnae ask the lassie out can ye bloody well get on with it? I need a wee.

Billy Right I should probably, um.

Billy hesitates and turns to leave.
 A game of missed glances. Crea watches Billy leave, until she turns away. Billy glances back at her.

Crea (*whispers to Tersia*) You've got a catheter in. So if you need a wee you can just let it go.

Tersia Ahhh. That's much better. So it is.

1.3

Ani is on the phone, which is ringing out, holding a stack of IVs.
 Crea parks Tersia close to the nurses' station, where she can be kept an eye on.

Crea Another glorious night to be alive.

Ani Hi Crea.

Crea I didn't see you take your handover.

Ani Oh, I took my handover in the staff toilet.

Beat.

Sophie was a bit, um, emotional.

Crea Dayshift was heavy. Onwards and upwards.

Beat.

Right. Quick safety brief. There's a hole in the ceiling.

Ani Yeah I noticed.

Crea I'll set up some safety cones. No one is to be within a metre of it.

Ani Got it.

Crea What are your numbers?

Ani I've got twelve patients in this quarter, over a maximum of eight. Ten are bed-waits.

Crea There's not much movement through the hospital. If you need to escalate anything to the medical staff, you'll go next door.

Ani That's fine. But is there another nurse on with me on this side?

Crea We're short. You're the most experienced on, so I've left you on your own in here. I'll come in to cover your breaks.

Ani It's just.

Crea Is there a problem?

Ani It's the guy in Bed Four. Intracranial haemorrhage. The doctors will soon make him palliative. They think it will be quick and he could pass tonight. I've been trying to find him a bed somewhere quieter, no joy. He's not got any family with him, and I can't seem to get in touch with anyone.

Crea That's unfortunate.

Ani If I'm on my own here. I'm just worried he'll. You know.

Crea Our numbers aren't great tonight, Ani.

Ani No one should die alone.

Crea I've assigned a student to you as well. She should be here any minute.

Ani Tell me they're a final-year hotshot that can work independently.

A loud crash. Student Nurse Lina enters, having walked into a bin.

Lina Ow!

Crea (*whispers*) Lina is repeating her first year on probation on account of causing a major incident.
The uni want us to give an opinion as to whether they should keep her on.

Ani Fantastic.

Lina Hiya!

Crea Are you chewing gum?

Lina Um yeah but like it helps with my anxiety . . .

Crea Spit it out. The bin's over there.

Lina But –

Crea Now.

Lina sighs and takes her time spitting out her gum. It's an ordeal.

(*To Ani.*) Is there anyone you're particularly worried about?

Ani On Trolley Four I've got Isla. Young girl with extensive bruising having fallen from a height. She's stable. But I don't know. There's something about her.

Lina returns. Crea motions for her to 'write this down'; she does.

Bed Five. Turnbull. Foreign object to gluteus maximus. Which is fitting because. He's a total –

Ani looks at Lina and holds her tongue.

You'll see when you met him. I guarantee you he will put in a complaint.
And over there is Tersia Sibyl, seventy-eight. Came in with a urinary tract infection and a fall at home. Restless. Pyrexic. Delirious. IV antibiotics. Probably a one-to-one.

Crea That's fine. I'll see to those three myself when I can. That will buy you a bit of time with the man in Bed Four.

Ani Okay. Thanks.

Crea Lina. This is a probationary shift. You'll be working under Staff Nurse Ani. Please work within the limits of your skill set and use your initiative.

Beat.

Get your hair off your collar, Ani.

Crea exits.
Ani pulls her hair higher. Lina rolls her eyes.

Lina What a cow. Am-i-rite?

Ani Do you realise who that was?

Lina Um. No.

Ani That was our Senior Charge Nurse. The High Priestess. Back in the day we would have all had to stand when she entered the room.

Lina I thought she was a bit rude to be honest.

Ani You did, did you?

Lina Um.

Ani There are some people that quietly hold the whole world together.

That woman could run a continent. Show some respect.

Lina Oh no oh no oh no.
(*Hitting her head.*) Stupid stupid stupid!

Ani Whoa. Calm down.

Lina Omigod. I've messed this up already.

Ani It's fine. Just take a deep breath.

Lina I'm sorry. Uh. Hi. I'm Lina.

Ani Hi Lina.

Lina My preceptor says I should give this note to every nurse that agrees to take charge of me. It's just an account of the, um. Incident.

Ani (*reads the note*) Wow. They, uh, kept you on after that?

Lina Just to say I've done a lot of reflecting and I'm like totally ready to move on.

Ani Okay, well. Why don't you go over to the drugs cupboard, have a look at all the drugs in there, take a note of their indications and contraindications.

Lina Okay. It's just.

Ani Is there a problem?

Lina It's just that the last nurse that I worked with also just took one look at me and told me to go to the drugs cupboard. She seemed super stressed as well.

Ani I'm not stressed.

Beat.

I am not stressed.

Lina My main feedback so far is that I 'need prompting'. Everyone just keeps ticking the same box, so it's all just like 'needs prompting', 'needs prompting'. Tonight is probably my last chance at being a nurse. The charge nurse said to use my initiative. But like it's hard to show initiative if I'm not allowed to touch anything. Or anyone.

Ani Okay. I'll give you one job. Do you know how to set up a nebuliser?

Lina (*has no idea*) One hundred per cent.

Ani Over the course of the night, I'll need a few nebulisers. When I need one, I will flag you down and supervise you to administer it.

Lina That would be. Amazing.

Ani Other than that. You're going to be stationed in there.

A flicker of hesitation.

Here are the keys to the drugs cupboard. Don't touch the red one. Whatever you do. Don't lose them.

Lina Thanks. I really want to be a nurse. All I've ever wanted to do is help people.

Ani The road to hell is paved with good intentions.

Lina You won't regret this.

Act Two

2.1A

During the scene below, Ani checks in on Mr Hopper. She finds him asleep in the chair. She places a cup of cold milk in front of him.

We see her in and out of the cubicles, tending to other patients. She calls the number on file for Mr Hopper's next-of-kin. The number is no longer in service.

2.1B

We hear the low groaning of Turnbull in pain.

Turnbull is inside a cubicle in Pod B, lying prone on a stretcher. The end of a comedically large metal spike protrudes from his bum cheek. Crea draws back his curtain and enters. She holds a glass of water, IV antibiotics and some IV morphine.

Turnbull It's about bloody time.

Crea Could you confirm your name and date of birth for me?

Turnbull Turnbull. 2nd of March 1958.
Five hours and forty-two minutes I've been waiting. With this thing in my arse.
Not so much as a Jelly Baby for sustenance.

Crea You've done very well, Mr Turnbull.

Turnbull I was due pain relief seven minutes ago.

Crea Here's the plan. I'm going to insert a cannula to give you some antibiotics. I'll then have look at your backside, see if I can manage to extract the spike myself and give you some morphine. All goes according to plan, I'll clean and dress the wound and you'll be on your way shortly after. Any questions?

Turnbull Just bloody get on with it.

Crea applies a tourniquet to Turnbull's arm and begins cannulation. She proceeds precisely as she's stated above.

I take it you're the nurse in charge. Things must be busy if you're on the floor.

Crea It is what it is.

Turnbull This hospital was in the newspaper the other day.

Crea I'm aware.

Turnbull There was a big picture of the front of this department, your department, on the cover.
The word SHAMBLES over the top in capital letters.

Crea This site has been running at maximum capacity since March 2020.

Turnbull Very informative article. People deserve to know that this service is failing.

Crea The department is not in its prime, I'll give you that.

Turnbull Shambles. That's what it is. The state of this place. Shambles is putting it kindly.

Crea Thanks for your feedback.

Turnbull This National Health Service. I wish they would just do away with it once and for all.

Crea Be careful what you wish for.

Turnbull Let the whole thing crumble to the ground. Lance it like a pus-filled blister.

Crea Speaking of which. Let's have a look at your bahookie.

She examines the damage.

So how exactly did you manage this, Mr Turnbull?

Turnbull Well. I've been preparing these metal spikes for my fence, to keep intruders out of my back garden. There was some ice, And. Then I just – (*Swoosh, bam.*) The thing went right into my arse.

Crea What a pity.

Turnbull Indeed.

Crea We get a lot of foreign object in rectum. But foreign object in bum cheek is a rarity.

Turnbull Foreign object in rectum! The world is full of degenerates. Sometimes, you know, you just stop and you look around and you think to yourself. All these people coming over and it's not what it used to be. Oh it's all gone so horribly wrong. And the people in that waiting room. I despair.

Crea opens a sterile dressing pack and prepares to extract the protrusion.

Crea What's that smell. Is that lavender?

Turnbull Well yes.

Crea I love the smell of lavender. So invigorating.

Turnbull According to the internet they don't like lavender.

Crea Who?

Turnbull The intruders.

Beat.

So I put some on lavender oil on the spike.

Crea So you lubricated the shaft with lavender oil. And its now ended up in your bum cheek.

Turnbull Ohhh. Oh Christ. You're not implying that I was seeking some sort of. Degenerate gratification. Ugh.

Crea Oh no. I'm not implying anything, Mr Turnbull.

Turnbull The cats were crapping on my cabbages.

Crea The service is entirely non-judgemental, from cradle to grave, 'made available to rich and poor alike in accordance with medical need and no other criteria'.

Turnbull My personal cabbages.

Crea I'll just give you a bit of morphine.

Turnbull waves consent.

That's it going in.

Crea administers the morphine

Turnbull Savoy cabbages.

Crea Had you maybe been round to have a word with the cat owners?

Turnbull (*the morphine starts to take effect*) Five hours and forty-six oooh. The numbers are spinning.
 (*Sings, slurring words.*) I can see what you're implying, but degenerate gratification is, quite simply woweee. No siree.

Crea Everything all right, Mr Turnbull?

Turnbull Oh. Yes yes. Well. Come to think of it. Quite pleasant actually.

Crea One-two-three.

Crea extracts the spike and puts pressure on the wound.

That's it done.

Once finished applying pressure, Crea dresses the wound.

Turnbull (*high*) I did. I did go round. To the new neighbours. To have words. I looked in the window. Fire was on. Soft glow. Young children. Mess, you know. Spilt yogurt on the kitchen floor. So full of life. Went to ring the doorbell and thought no. Mustn't. What if she invited me in for a cuppa. Who could be bothered with all of that, eh?

Starts with a small nod across the hedge, a one-off, who knows where one might end up.

Crea That's your wound all dressed, Mr Turnbull, your antibiotics are running through. A nurse will be back in an hour or so with some further pain relief.

She goes to bin the spike.

Turnbull Oh no. No no no. Don't bin that. I'll need that for my. For my.

Crea leaves the spike in the cubicle and exits.

2.2

Crea exits Turnbull's cubicle and heads for Tersia.
Tersia gazes up at the HOLE *in the ceiling. Particles fall like snow into the unit.*

Tersia (*to herself*) Endless darkness. Snowfall. Everything white and deathly still. Until –

Tersia is startled by Crea behind her changing a bag of fluids on her drip stand.

Crea Don't mind me, Tersia. I'm just having a check of your drugs.

Tersia Knock yourself out, hen. Ahm not here to judge.

Crea Can you tell me today's date and where you are just now?

Tersia It is Thursday the 21st of December.

Crea That's right.

Tersia It's Thursday 21st of December 1974. We're in the ladies' toilets of the Clouds Disco, above the Majestic Theatre. And tonight, will be a night that none of us will live to forget.

Crea You're in hospital with a urinary tract infection, Tersia. It's making you a bit confused.

Tersia You think I'm confused. Have you seen what you're wearing?

Crea This is my uniform.

Tersia Why is it so flat?

Crea I've got very good at ironing.

Tersia Too good.
  (*Pondering this, certain.*) Yes. That's the crux of the problem.
  She used to be good fun.

Crea checks Tersia's temperature with an ear probe, startling her.

Crea Just a wee check of your temperature.
  (*Reading the thermometer.*) Jesus.

Tersia Och. I know that lad.

Crea Which lad? Jesus?

  Crea administers some liquid paracetamol.

Tersia Oh. Aye. Quite a tasty little pork chop, isn't he? It's the way he carries himself. Sauntering about all draped in white. Real sense of style. I've never been one for contemporary menswear.

  Beat.

Ohh. That bit when he goes in and kicks over all the tables.

Crea The Cleansing of the Temple.

Tersia 'Get outta my house!' 'Get out!' This is a holy place.
  Mmm. That really does it for me. Not my number one, mind. But he is in my top five.
  (*Seeing Billy approach.*) Speaking of.

Tersia winks at Crea.
  At the sight of Billy, Crea might reflexively pat her hair into place.
  Billy enters pushing a wheelchair that carries young Isla, who has sustained an elbow fracture from a fall.

Billy Hi Crea. Just bringing this young lassie back from X-Ray.

Crea What was your name, sweetheart?

Isla Isla.

Crea She's fine there, Billy. I'll see to Isla in a wee moment.

Crea and Billy hold each other's gaze a moment too long.

Tersia I recognise you.

Billy From earlier, aye.

Tersia This wee boy comes to my play park. He climbs right up to the top of the big slide and he freezes. Shifts his weight. Overthinking it. Just take the plunge, son! Take the bloomin' plunge.

Billy I ought to crack on.

Tersia Suit yourself, son. Tick tock.

Billy hesitates, then exits.
  Crea takes a pair of safety socks out of her pocket.

Crea I've brought you some safety socks.

Tersia Dear God.

Crea What's wrong?

Tersia They're hideous.

Crea Your boots are lovely but it would be safer if you could wear these for now.

Tersia Absolutely not.
  (*To Isla.*) Want some socks, kiddo?

Isla Um. No thanks.

Tersia She's wise.

Crea We'll come back to the socks.

Crea is about to exit. Tersia grabs her by the wrist.

Tersia Look at us. The whole gang together. One last night at the Clouds Disco.
We will look back on this night for the rest of our days.
And say: We were there. We were alive.
Pull yourselves together!
Look at the state of the two of you.
(*To Crea.*) She's dressed like a pancake.
(*To Isla.*) And, you.
Oh!
Oh dear God.

Tersia looks deep into Isla's eyes and is silenced by what she sees.
 She continues to stare. It unnerves Crea.
 Isla finally looks away.
 Tersia in turn shuts her eyes and seems to drift off to sleep.
 Crea waits a moment, then begins to gently peel off Tersia's glittery boots and replaces them with the safety socks. Tersia doesn't notice.
 Crea looks up at Isla and winks at her.
 In the background we see Billy enter, hesitate and exit.
 Billy re-enters. That's it. He's going in for the kill this time.

Billy Crea, I've brought you some coffee.

Crea Oh. Um. Cheers, Billy.

Billy What are you doing Saturday?

Crea Saturday. I'm. Um.

Billy Never quite got the timing right. Maybe it's. Shut up, Billy.

Crea No. Don't shut up, Billy, I'm free on Saturday.

Billy Great.

Crea Grand.

Billy exits.

2.3

Crea attempts to seamlessly transition to the care of Isla. Isla is having none of it.
   Makeshift wound dressings cover her wrists, elbows and knees.

Isla Sooooo. Is that your boyfriend?

Crea Oh. No. Just a friend.

Isla Uh-huh.

Crea Sorry. That was unprofessional.

Isla Don't be sorry. That's the best thing that's happened in here all day.
   Not bad for an old guy.

Crea It's been a long time coming.

Beat.

Right. Let's have a look. I'll clean up these wounds.

Crea whips out a sterile dressing pack and proceeds to undress the bandages on Isla's arm. At the sight of the wound, Isla flinches and appears stricken.
   Crea notices this. She hands Isla her phone.

Crea Okay. Do me a favour. Choose me an outfit for Saturday.

Isla Okay.

Crea Something casual, with a bit of, you know –

Isla Rizz.

Crea Is that what the kids are calling it these days?

Isla It's short for charisma.

Crea Very innovative.

Isla . . . Definitely wear the blue.

Crea You think?

Isla One hundred per cent. And you should paint your nails. A deep dark Merlot.

Crea I don't bother with nail varnish. I'm in here that often.

Isla I thought you said it was a long time coming.

Crea Fair enough. Sounds like a plan.

Beat.

I've seen you in here before.

Isla I hope I'm not a regular.

Crea So how'd you manage all this?

Isla Um. There's this place, by the sea, that I like to go. Um, for some peace. I was just climbing up to the bit that I like. And, um. There was a dog walker going past and she shouted up at me. I guess it kind of spooked me and I fell. It's just my knee and my elbow, a few scratches. A bit silly really. I'm fine.

Crea It doesn't look fine. You must have been high up.

Isla It's no big deal.

Crea We'll await the results of your X-ray. There might be a bit of a wait.

Isla That's okay.

Crea Does someone know you're in here?

Isla The lady walking her dog brought me in. She sat with me the entire time we were in the waiting room.

Crea What about your parents? Your friends?

Isla It's all right. I'm a big girl.

Crea How old are you?

Isla Almost twenty.

Crea Not as big as you think.

Tersia sits bolt upright and is staring into Isla's eyes in trepidation.

Tersia Bette.

Crea Don't mind her. It's just the delirium.

Isla waves at Tersia weakly.

Isla I could never do what you do.

Crea Never say never.

Isla You must really have it together.

Crea Nursing attracts all sorts. Some of the best nurses have been a wee bit broken themselves.

Isla I'm not just a wee bit broken.

Crea's pager goes. It's important. Crea silences it.

Crea What do you mean by that?

Isla Nothing. You can get that. It's probably important.

Crea You're important.

Isla might roll her eyes.

I like your nails.

Isla Thanks. I picked them out especially.

The pager bleeps again.

I'm fine. Honestly. You can get that.

Crea I'm going to have to. I'm going to come back and we're going to finish this conversation, okay?

Isla Sure.

A clump of roof falls to the floor expanding the HOLE *in the ceiling.*
  Isla gazes at the HOLE, *possessed by a thought.*
  Mr Hopper tries to ignore it.

2.4

Mr Hopper is awake. He is savouring the cup of cold milk that Ani left for him.
  Ani enters, pushing in a hospital bed.

Ani Mr Hopper?

Mr Hopper Iain. Call me Iain.

Ani Would you like to speak with the hospital chaplain?

Mr Hopper Nah. I've got you looking after me. And this is the best cup of cold milk I've ever had in my life.
  What would I need a chaplain for?

Ani I've been calling around the hospital, trying to find you a bed somewhere quieter. But it might be that this is the best we can do for now.

Mr Hopper It doesn't matter.

Ani It does matter. I've brought this hospital bed through for you. Just a bit more comfortable. Could I give you a hand getting in?

Mr Hopper You're all right. I'll manage.

Mr Hopper stands too suddenly. He wavers unsteadily. Ani steadies him as he comes to.

Ani Whoa. Easy.

Ani guides him as he steps towards the bed.

Mr Hopper Could be worse though.

Ani Could it?

Mr Hopper Than the likes of you trying to get me into bed.

Ani That was terrible.

Mr Hopper It was. Terrible.

Ani Bed's behind you.

Mr Hopper crashes down onto the bed. Ani calmly swings his legs into the bed.

I brought you a gown. I'll let you change into that yourself.

Mr Hopper blacks out. He's swinging in and out of consciousness with increasing frequency.

Mr Hopper? I'm going to shine this torch in your eyes.

Ani checks his pupils. He comes to.

Mr Hopper Just a blackout.

Ani I take it you've spoken to the consultant.

Mr Hopper She's not long gone. She showed me the scan. The shadow.

Ani What is your understanding of what's happening to you?

Mr Hopper See, the doc was making a big deal of it. But Ah've been having these blackouts for ages now and . . .

Ani Iain, your prognosis is really poor.

Mr Hopper Let's not blow things out of proportion. I'll stay the night, I'll put the gown and all. But I'll be away after that.

Beat.

Ani The doctor doesn't think you'll make it through the night.

Beat.

Mr Hopper And you. What do you think?

Ani I've known that consultant for a long time now. She's never wrong.

Mr Hopper waves his hand dismissively.

Mr Hopper I'll be fine.

Ani Do you want to know what I think? I think you need to face that you've not got much time left, because there's nothing we can do to change that.

Silence. A ripple of the BILLOWING CURTAIN.
Mr Hopper laughs. And laughs.

Mr Hopper (*tries to speak through peals of laughter*) One year tomorrow. I'll have been stone cold sober. Thought the drink would be the death of me, only to be struck down by something else entirely. Classic. What a belter.

Ani I tried to get in touch with your wife.

Mr Hopper That'd be my ex-wife.

Ani You were asleep. It was the only number we had on file.

Mr Hopper Leave it.

Ani The number was no longer in service.

Mr Hopper Please just leave me.

Ani You'll want someone here with you tonight.

Mr Hopper We're born alone. We die alone.

Ani No one's ever actually born alone, are they? I don't think anyone should die alone.

Mr Hopper I said leave it!

Ani Fine.

Ani turns to leave.
   The CURTAIN BILLOWS. A wave of pure terror ripples through Mr Hopper.
   Just as Ani is about to exit:

Mr Hopper . . . Nurse?

Ani Yes?

Mr Hopper I'm scared.

Ani I know. You're not alone. I'll be back as soon as I can.

Ani exits Mr Hopper's bedspace.

2.5

Crea meets Ani.

Crea Did you manage to get some time with the man in Bed Four?

Ani Yes, but –

Crea Good. Onwards and upwards.

Ani It's just that –

Crea Ani. I've been meaning to say. I suppose this is as good a time as any. You're a good nurse.

Ani Thank you. That means a lot to me. Coming from you.

Crea We've decided to open another Charge Nurse position here. To work directly under myself. I think you'd be an excellent candidate.

Ani Oh wow. I, um.

Crea I thought you'd be over the moon.

Ani I am. I'm just.

Crea On a Band Six salary you could get a mortgage. Move somewhere closer, so you wouldn't have that awful commute. When I think of the future of this unit, Ani. I think of you. You're a steady pair of hands.

Ani Thanks. I'll definitely. Um. Think about applying.

Crea Good. I can't lose another nurse to selling pictures of her feet on the internet.

Ani Seems to pay her bills.

Crea (*part-joking*) That's the problem with your generation, Ani. There's more to life than me time and foot selfies.

Crea's pager beeps.

I need to go.

Ani Crea. The man in Bed Four. I'd like to go back and spend more time with him.

Crea (*checks her pager*) What about the student?

Ani The student is. Just. No.

Beat.

He's still conscious. He's terrified. And alone.

Crea I can see you're concerned. But you have other patients under your care. I appreciate it's not ideal.

Ani No. It isn't.

Crea I'm doing the best I can here.

Ani I just want to feel like a nurse for once.

Crea I'm afraid it's a matter of prioritisation.

Ani No.

Silence.

Crea Excuse me?

Ani No one should die alone. I've done that during the pandemic. I'm not doing it again.

Crea You're a registered nurse, Ani. You'll need to meet the pressures of your caseload.

Ani I'm aware of that.

Crea We have a duty of care to all patients in this department. You're not to spend any further time in that bedspace until the needs of all the other patients in this base have been met in a safe and timely manner. Is that understood?

NMC PANEL HEARING: SECTION TWO

A shift.

Nursing and Midwifery Council (NMC) Hearing. The linens cupboard transforms into a boardroom, from where the NMC Panel Chair speaks into a desktop microphone. A light shines down from the HOLE *onto Ani. Ani remains in the world of the play while addressing the NMC Panel Chair.*

Ani Ani Stevens. Registration Number S0453101X.

NMC Panel Chair Charge Nurse Crea Harrower was your former line manager?

Ani That is correct.

NMC Panel Chair And what was your relationship like with Charge Nurse Crea Harrower?

Ani Good. It was good.

NMC Panel Chair You wrote in your statement that you had a disagreement on the night in question.

Ani It seemed important at the time, but on reflection, I don't think it's relevant.

NMC Panel Chair You had a disagreement with your line manager on a shift that ended in an untimely and avoidable death. I assure you, it's relevant.

Ani Can I just ask, just out of curiosity, when was the last time you worked in front line care?

NMC Panel Chair Ms Stevens.

Ani Just curious.

NMC Panel Chair What was your relationship like with Charge Nurse Harrower?

Ani When I first joined the unit, Nurse Harrower was assigned to be my mentor. I followed her around like a puppy and wrote down everything she said and how she said it. So much of what we know in nursing is learned from other nurses. Crea was calm, competent, meticulous. Nothing would go by her. She had a way with people. A laugh would ring through the unit. A way of having a million jobs to do, but all the time in the world.

Crea believed in the principle of health care made available to rich and poor alike on the basis of medical need and no other criteria. Like many nurses of her generation, she believed that nursing wasn't just a job. That it was a calling. A vocation. My generation isn't like that. Of course it's a job . . . I mean? Isn't it?

NMC Panel Chair Ms Stevens if you could focus on –

Ani When she was appointed Senior Charge Nurse, she had plans for the place. Real plans. The world had other plans. Around that time, we started haemorrhaging staff. The unit was stretched, and will remain stretched, for a very long time. This took its toll.

NMC Panel Chair Ms Stevens. If you could ensure your statement is relevant to the night in question.

Ani I assure you it's relevant. Crea held the unit together – through the pandemic and its aftermath. If a shift remained unfilled, she would come in and fill it herself, as she had on the night in question.

NMC Panel Chair You had a disagreement that night.

Ani Yeah. We did.

I am aware that Crea Harrower has stated that she assumes full responsibility for the untimely and avoidable death that occurred under our care. But I hope that my version of events would call that statement into question.

Act Three

3.1

Ani hesitates. She decides to disobey Crea's instructions and return to Mr Hopper's cubicle. Mr Hopper has changed into a hospital gown. He sits awake in the hospital bed.
Ani applies ECG stickers and connects Mr Hopper to some monitoring cables.

Mr Hopper So this is how it ends, eh. To the sound of Smooth Radio in a windowless room.

Ani I can change the radio station.

Mr Hopper The radio is the least of my problems.

Mr Hopper smiles. Ani meets his smile.

Ani Do you live with anyone, Iain?

Mr Hopper Just me in my bedsit. Going about my business. Guess I'm a bit of a hermit.

Ani It's funny. You don't seem like the type.

Mr Hopper I've got a sponsor. I don't want to bog them down with all this.

Ani I don't want to labour the point. There must be someone.

Mr Hopper Please. Just (leave it).

Ani Maybe someone from your past.

Mr Hopper I've asked you to leave it! What do you not understand?

Beat.

Ani My dad died alone. In hospital. We weren't on good terms. Maybe I should have tried harder to get there sooner. I don't know. There's a guilt I wouldn't wish on anyone.

I often think about the nurse that was on shift that day, caring for him. I like to think they were gentle. I like to think they took the time.

This bleed could go at any moment.

Beat.

Mr Hopper I have a son.
There's a number in my, uh, wallet –

Ani picks up his trousers and looks through the pocket.

Help yourself to a sweetie.

Ani Thanks.

Ani finds the number and shows him.

Mr Hopper That's it.

Beat.

Do you think it's too late?

Ani I don't know.

Mr Hopper But you need to tell him. You need to tell him that –

A shudder from the BILLOWING CURTAIN.
Mr Hopper blacks out in terror. The monitoring that Ani has just placed on him begins to alarm. His oxygen saturations are perilously low.
Ani slips a high concentration oxygen mask onto her patient that she had prepared at his bedside.

Ani Nice slow deep even breaths.

Mr Hopper Tell him that –

Ani Shhh . . .

Mr Hopper And tell him –
Just ask him to come.

Ani I will.

Ani exits Mr Hopper's bedspace.

3.2

Having just exited Mr Hopper's bedspace, Ani finds Tersia up on her feet stumbling towards the HOLE *in the ceiling. We can now see the night sky.*

Ani immediately puts down her notes and Mr Hopper's son's number and rushes to steady Tersia.

Tersia Everything white and deathly still. Then from the furthest corners most unexpected –

Ani Where are you off to, Tersia?

Tersia Shhh! Come look!

Ani There's a hole in the ceiling. It's not ideal.

Tersia No. Look. Look up from here. From right here! You can see just the edge of the glitter ball. Soon it will be directly upon us.

Ani It's the moon.

Tersia Don't be ridiculous.

Beat.

Oh, it's you. The one who runs in circles.

Ani That's me.

Tersia From darkness we emerge and to darkness we return. For one brief moment we are conductors of the light.

Ani Why don't you come back here and have a wee seat.

Tersia is compliant as Ani guides her back to a safe, seated position.
Ani gives her a cup of cold water.

How about a nice cold glass of water?

Tersia She who runs in circles. Trying to keep everything in its place. She's up against the tide.

Ani Lina!

Lina Yes?

Ani I'm behind on my IVs. I need you to keep a close eye on Tersia and watch the floor.

Lina Me?

Beat.

I mean. Great. I'm totally ready for this. I was. Born ready.

Ani If anyone needs something *very* basic, like a glass of water, or to be shown where the toilet is, you can go ahead and do that. Anything more complicated –

Lina Anything more complicated, I'll just use my initiative.

Ani Absolutely not. If there's anything more complicated, I want you to come and get me. Understood?

Lina Like one hundred per cent.

Ani exits. A look of panic on Lina's face.

Um –

Ani prepares her IV medications in the drugs cupboard. She weaves in and out of the cubicles to administer them.
Lina moves out to stand in front of the staff base.
Tersia has caught sight of where her glittery boots have been stashed nearby and swipes them. She makes eye contact with Lina, defiant.
Lina looks away.

Tersia begins to remove her safety socks and put the heels back on.
Lina pretends not to notice until she can't anymore. She builds up the courage to intervene.

Lina Um. Are you like meant to be wearing those?

Tersia Yes.

Lina Maybe you would be safer in the safety socks.

Tersia Oh I'm much better in these. Believe me.

Lina I guess it's patient-centred care?

Tersia Don't worry about me, love. Worry about your eyebrows.

Tersia rises to her feet with ease. Lina rushes to her side.

Lina Whoa! Um.

Tersia dances a jig. She's steady as ever in the heels.

Tersia Safety first.

Tersia wanders with the drip stand.
Lina follows her.

Lina Maybe you should just like sit down and like relax.

Tersia Oh, I can't relax, doll.

Lina Why not?

Tersia I have waited my whole life for this moment, and I am going to look sensational.

Lina You do. But –

Tersia And see, if we're talking woman to woman. I need a shit.

Lina Oh. Um. Yeah! That I can help with. The toilets are that way. Wait. I think they might actually be that way. Oh! Oh wait. I think you might like need like one of those toilets on wheels that I could like bring to you but I'm not sure where they are.

Tersia Thanks love that's dead clear.

Turnbull (*off*) Hellooooo?? Helloooooooo??

Lina (*calling back*) One second!

Lina Wait. Do you like need a hand?

Tersia Don't be ridiculous.

Lina Um. But!

Turnbull (*off*) Hellooooooo???

Lina Just coming!

Lina heads for Turnbull's cubicle as:
   Tersia saunters across the stage, stops at the HOLE *and gazes up at it.*
   Tersia walks over to the workstation. She swings a swivel chair around.

Tersia Ah. Toilet on wheels she said. Good lass.

During the scene below, Tersia proceeds to evacuate her bowels on the chair on wheels. She somehow makes this look graceful. She uses notes, including the number for Mr Hopper's son, to wipe herself.
   Meanwhile:
   Lina enters Turnbull's cubicle.
   He is still lying prone, recovering from the spike extraction.

Lina Um. Hello. My name is Lina and I'm a student nurse.

Turnbull I'm in a lot of pain.

Lina Um. Would you like a glass of water?

Turnbull I was due pain medication seven minutes ago.

Lina Um. Everyone is sort of like busy at the moment.

Turnbull Well, are you busy?

Lina Um not really no.

Turnbull Well can you get me some pain relief?

Lina Um. Well. Like. I'm just a student. But I can tell the nurse. She's on a meds round and I think someone is just like dying. So.

Turnbull Well that bodes well.

Lina Um. Would you like a glass of water or to be shown where the toilet is?

Turnbull No. I would like some pain relief.

Lina Okay. No problem. Just give me two minutes. I'm going to go and get the nurse.

Lina is pleased with herself. She looks out into the corridor and sees Tersia evacuating her bowels.
Lina freezes. She turns back into the cubicle, much to Turnbull's bafflement. She peeks her head out of the curtain and sees Ani returning. She decides to hide in Turnbull's cubicle, trying to appear casual to him.
She might eat a stick of gum. She might offer some to Turnbull.
Meanwhile, Ani returns to the nurses' station. She opens her second can of energy drink. She picks up the phone and Mr Hopper's son's number and begins to dial.
She sniffs.
She sees the excrement on it.

Tersia This loo roll is like sandpaper.

Ani sees Tersia.

Ani Oh dear. Let's get you freshened up.
(*Calls.*) Lina? Lina???

Lina continues to hide in Turnbull's cubicle.

Where has that student gone?

Lina backs into the drugs cupboard to hide.

Tersia Circles. Where are you taking me, love?

Ani Big night ahead. I want to make sure you're sparkling.

Tersia Quite right. Not sure about these facilities though. Two stars. That's all you'll get from me. Two stars.

Ani wheels Tersia aside to be cleaned in privacy.

3.3

A reverie. The calm before the storm.
 A light snow begins to fall from the HOLE.
 We see Mr Hopper in his bed, contemplating his life from his deathbed. He is taunted by the BILLOWING CURTAIN.
 Crea stands in front of a computer screen, managing the unit. It's high-stakes Tetris. She moves coloured boxes representing the floor plan of the department. She has three phones in front of her and speaks into them alternately.
 A moment of tenderness as Ani washes Tersia. Tersia notices she is soiled and feels revulsion. Ani sings to distract her from this. Tersia may join in.
 We hear (and may see the figure of) Isla singing separately.
 Crea's phone calls are added into the soundscape, interspersed with queue updates from the unit phone and Turnbull's calls for help.

Crea (*on phone*) Predicted bed requests overnight. Twelve medical beds, eight surgical, four psych, three HDU, two ICU. The chap that dismembered the cat went tonto. Absconded. Missing person protocol.

Unit Phone Your call is important to us. You are number sixty-seven in the queue.

Turnbull Hellooo?????

Crea (*on phone*) Well I've got six patients in imaginary bedspaces in the name of continuous flow.
 Oh I've heard he's really good. I tried to get an appointment for my roots, but the line is always busy and I don't know, I've gone off being on the phone.

Unit Phone Your call is important to us. You are number sixty-seven in the queue.

Turnbull Helloooooooooo???

Crea (*on phone*) Oh, no, there is an actual hole. I can see the sky.

Pause.

What have I personally done about it? Have I mixed the cement?
 It's been cordoned off and risk assessed. I'm on hold with the contractor. The estates department would have –

Pause.

Right, okay. That should be fine as long as the Resus phone doesn't ring.

The Resusitation phone rings.

Bugger.

This rhythm continues to build, but sits under the text in 3.4, 3.5, 3,6 and 3.7, until it bursts through and permeates everything in 3.8.

3.4

Ani returns with Tersia, who is back in the safety socks. Ani places some headphones on Tersia and stashes her boots in the staff base, where Lina is scrubbing down surfaces with ferocity.

Ani Oh. There you are. I was looking for you. Where did you go?

Lina Oh. I was just like assisting another patient.

Ani Everything okay?

Lina Yeah. I like one hundred per cent sorted them out. Then I thought I'd just like. Do some cleaning. You know.

Ani Okay.

Ani parks Tersia by the nurses' station. She starts to search for the notes with Mr Hopper's son's number.

(*Unable to find it and beginning to panic.*) Oh. Oh God. Oh fuck.

Lina Is everything okay?

Ani You didn't throw anything out did you?

Lina Um. No.

Ani You didn't see a soiled bit of paper with a telephone number.

Lina Oh that. Yeah. I, um, tried to salvage that. I wiped it down as best I could with antiseptic wipes, but it was pretty soiled so I decided to bin it, but then I was like maybe it's important, so I like stuck it right at the top of the bin just in case.

Lina points to the number in the bin.

Ani Omigod. Lina, you're brilliant.

Lina I . . . ? I am?

Ani Good work. It's great to see you using your initiative.

Lina (*entire existence validated*) Um. Thanks. Thank you so much.

Lina glows.
Ani turns and dials the cleaned but still stained phone number of Mr Hopper's son.

Ani Oh. Hi there. Who am I speaking to?

Pause.

My name is Ani. I'm a nurse in the Accident and Emergency Department at Almondvale Hospital. I'm calling about your dad, Mr Iain Hopper?

Voice on phone says: 'I'm not interested.'

Oh. Um. Your father is severely unwell. He's suffered a serious bleed to the brain. His prognosis is very poor. I wondered if you wanted to come and –

Voice on phone says: 'I said I'm not interested!'

He wanted to tell you something. But I couldn't make out –

The phone has been put down.

Um, hello?

Pause.

Hello?

Ani puts the phone down and sighs.
Lina continues cleaning furiously.

Ani The man in Bed Four. It looks like he's going to pass tonight.

Lina Omigod. Like actually?

Ani Yeah. Like actually. I'm going to go sit with him for just a few minutes. I've given Tersia my headphones, hopefully she'll settle. Is there anything else you need before I head in there?

Lina No. I've totally got this.

Ani Good.

*Ani enters Mr Hopper's bedspace.
Beat.*

Turnbull (*off*) Helloooooooo???

Lina Fuck.

3.5

Scenes 3.5a and 3.5b should be played semi-simultaneously. Scene 3.5b may commence when Lina heads for the drugs cupboard.

3.5A

Turnbull (*off*) Heeeeellloooooo????

Lina confidently enters Turnbull's bedspace.

I'm in pain here! This place is a disgrace.

Lina I'm going to get you that pain relief, Mr Turnbull.

Turnbull Well bloody get on with it then.

Lina I am going to use my initiative.

Lina heads for the drugs cupboard, talking to herself.

Nebulisers. I can do nebulisers.
She said don't touch the green key. Okay.

She opens a copy of the British National Formulary (BNF) and finds a nebuliser.

Wow! It's misting!!

Soon several nebulisers are on and misting away as she mutters, struggling with the keys to the drugs cupboard.

She creates a concoction while thumbing her way through the BNF.

Oh. Here. No one can read that handwriting.
Analgesia is a painkiller.
I'm using my initiative.

3.5B

Ani enters Mr Hopper's bedspace.

Mr Hopper Did you get through to my son?

Ani Um. Yeah.

Mr Hopper Did you tell him? Did you tell him that – ?

Mr Hopper is short of breath.

Ani Shhh. Yes. I spoke to him.

Silence.

Mr Hopper Maybe it was a bad idea.

Ani No, um. He said . . .

Beat.

(*Lying.*) He said he's going to try to make it in.

Mr Hopper Really?

Ani . . . Yeah.

Mr Hopper He said he'd come.

Ani Yeah.

Mr Hopper I've made mistakes.

Ani I'm not here to judge.

Mr Hopper I could never get the balance right between dream and reality.

Ani I think I know what you mean.

Mr Hopper I had this fantasy. I ran it over and over in my mind every day.

My boy. I was going to take him camping. Once I'd made it a whole year. I planned every detail. The tools. The route. The sausages. It'd be just me and my boy. Under the stars.

Ani He's probably on his way right now. I should –

Mr Hopper appears to be dozing off.
The CURTAIN BILLOWS. *He shudders.*

Mr Hopper Aah!

Ani stands between him and the wayward CURTAIN *and takes his hand.*

Ani Shh . . . That's it. You go to sleep.

3.5C

Lina attempts to get Ani's attention to check the medication she's prepared. Unable to do so, she decides to carry on.

Turnbull (*off*) Heeeeellloooooo????

Lina (*muttering to herself*) I'm coming already.

Lina holds the nebuliser, swinging the misting oxygen mask like an altar boy swinging a thurible or chain censer of frankincense. She stumbles down the hallway, misting the entire area with vaporised ketamine.
She arrives at Turnbull's cubicle. Mist flowing everywhere.

Turnbull It's about bloody time.

Lina Just one minute.

Turnbull What are you wating for?

Lina I just need the nurse to double check.

Both Turnbull and Lina begin to feel extremely light-headed.

I couldn't quite read the chart but it definitely said fifty, and this is fifty milligrams of analgesia for Fred Turnbull. The medication is perfectly in-date and it is.

She reads the label:

Ketamine.

Lina realises her error.
She looks for Ani who's still with Mr Hopper. She stumbles off to find Crea.

Lina Um. I should get help.

She stumbles again and nearly collapses as she heads off.

Turnbull Oh for Christ's sake.

Beat.

Oh wow. Wowee.

3.5D

Mr Hopper appears to be sleeping peacefully.
Ani tries to extract herself and sneak away.
His breathing has slowed. She stands over him to check the rise and fall of his chest.
Mr Hopper opens his eyes suddenly.
Ani shrieks.

Ani Ah!

Mr Hopper Ah!

Ani Ah! Sorry. You just gave me a fright.

Mr Hopper Still here. Still got it.

Ani I need to get back to the floor.

Mr Hopper Sure.

Beat.

Nurse?

Beat.

Never mind. You need to get on.

Ani What is it?

Mr Hopper Could you take me to a window?

Ani There are no windows in this part of the department.

Mr Hopper I have this urge to see the stars, one last time. You know that way the moonlight touches the clouds?

Ani I'm sorry.

Mr Hopper It's all right. I can feel a breeze.

Ani That's just because there's a hole in the ceiling.

Mr Hopper Could you take me to it?

Ani No. I can't. It's not safe.

Mr Hopper (*laughs*) What good is safe to me?

Ani I could lose my job.

Mr Hopper I understand.

Ani Which wouldn't be the worst thing.

Mr Hopper You get on. You've got things you need to do.

Ani Yeah there's always a million things I need to do.

Mr Hopper I've been enough bother. He's coming. My boy.

Ani One last glimpse of the stars.

Ani decides to push Mr Hopper under the HOLE. *She prepares to move bed out into the main space.*

3.6

During 3.5d, Tersia has reclaimed her boots from the staff base, and changed into them.

Tersia Deathly still. And then from the furthest corners most unexpected.

We hear Isla singing. She enters.

Bette. There you are.

Isla Oh. Um. I think you have me mistaken for someone else.

Tersia Don't belittle me.

Isla Just you might be getting muddled. My name is Isla.

Tersia I know exactly who you are. He's got this grip on you, Bette. And tonight we are going to –

Tersia wavers dangerously in her heels. Isla rushes to steady her, despite her own injuries.

Isla Whoa! I really don't think you should be wearing those boots.

Tersia Ahhh. Ah hah! Yes!
I'll take them off.

Tersia sits down and takes off the boots.

Isla Okay.

Tersia Yes! There's hope for us yet.

Tersia thrusts the boots at Isla.

You're absolutely right, Bette. You should wear them.

Isla Oh. No. Um.

Tersia Put them on.

Isla (*looking around desperately*) Where is the. Nurse.

Tersia Put them on or I will scream so loud I'll shatter every window in a five-mile radius so help us God.

Isla Okay. Okay.

At a loss, Isla decides she has no choice but to put the boots on.

Tersia Look at you. Beautiful.

Isla I'm really not.

Tersia The boots are all yours. That's my final will and testament.

Isla gazes up at the HOLE *in the ceiling. Tersia grabs her face suddenly and turns her away from it.*

When they discovered that the earth revolved around the sun, the whole world got their kickers in a twist. Talk of the town. When they discovered the enormity of the darkness, no one was all that surprised.

Turnbull (*off*) HELLOOOOO?????

Tersia Shhhhh . . . There are some real lookers in here tonight.

3.7

Turnbull's cubicle. A yellow packet of Jelly Babies sits just out of his reach.

Turnbull Hellooo . . .

Meow. Meow!

Not you! Pesky things.
Helllooooo.
No work ethic these days!

Tries unsuccessfully to reach the bag of Jelly Babies.

I can't reach my Jelly Babies.
HELLOOOOOO!!!

An apparition, 'Mary', enters. She wears a nursing uniform but there's something a bit sinister about her. She has a thick Northern accent and is jamming Jelly Babies into her mouth at an alarming rate.

'Mary' Hi, my name is Mary, I'm one of the muses that's going to be looking after you tonight.

Turnbull Oh thank God.

Beat.

The nurse is eating Jelly Babies at an alarming rate.

'Mary' The service is entirely non-judgemental, from cradle to grave, 'Made available to rich and poor alike in accordance with medical need and no other criteria.'

Turnbull Listen. You need to help me. My arse hurts and I think I might be hallucinating.

'Mary' Well let's have a look.

Inspecting Turnbull's arse.

Ooh. That does look sore.

Beat.

I'll have a look in my box of tricks . . .

'Mary' rummages through her pockets. 'Mary' whips out a large syringe filled with a coloured liquid.

Turnbull What . . . what is that?

'Mary' A bit of the ol' botulinum toxin, cut in with some sugar, glucose syrup, water, gelatine, cornflour, citric acid. And various colourings.

Turnbull Sounds legitimate.

'Mary' is nervous. She struggles with how to work the syringe.

. . . Are you a real nurse?

'Mary' No. I would have been, right. It's what I felt I wanted to do. But then the nursing bursary was cut. And I couldn't take on that debt, not for that pay. Domestic nursing applications in the UK are at an all-time low. Me? I went into aesthetics. I am deeply unfulfilled and bored out of my tits. But I'm debt free and me kids have nice trainers so.

Turnbull I am hallucinating.

'Mary' Listen. Don't get yourself in a tizz. The hypothetical me has been replaced by an AI assistant.

Turnbull Maybe this will sort it.

'Mary' Coco, help this man locate his sense of reality. (See ya later, babes.)

AI Assistant 'Coco' Coco will play 'Cat Themed Brain Rot'.

Coco plays 'Watermelon Meow Meow', or suchlike.

Turnbull Wait. Don't go. Coco, no. Coco, stop.
Help! I need help!
Please help me.
Helllooo??

Another apparition, 'Sindhu', enters. Fully scrubbed, she wears sterile gloves, a surgical gown and cap, and pushes a stainless-steel trolley. Like 'Mary', there's something not quite right about her appearance.

'Sindhu' What on earth is this terrible racket?

'Sindhu' turns the music off.

Turnbull Oh thank God.

'Sindhu' My name is Sindhu, I'm one of the muses that's going to be tending to you tonight.

'Sindhu' parks her trolley next to Turnbull. Turnbull, who had been resting on his side, rolls over onto his back. The apparition begins preparing a sterile field on his belly. A surgical lamp is switched on overhead.

Turnbull You're that student from earlier.

'Sindhu' Oh no, sir. I've long since graduated. Top of my class. Not that anyone's bothered. Or even asks.

Turnbull You need to help me. I seem to be losing my grip on reality.

'Sindhu' Reality is quite a nebulous concept.
Sharp scratch.

'Sindhu' uses a scalpel to make an incision in Turnbull's belly. She takes the scalpel away, bloodied, and begins to dig around in the wound with a pair of sterile forceps.
Turnbull is oblivious to this, disembodied.

Turnbull (*studying her face*) All of these faces. And I don't recognise any of them.

'Sindhu' 'All of these people. Coming over here.'

Turnbull I didn't mean you. It's just the green ones. And, well, some of the reds.

'Sindhu' Many of them recruited. To bolster a dwindling workforce.

Turnbull In fairness, the blackcurrant ones are my favourite.

'Sindhu' Ah, there we are.

'Sindhu' begins extracting glowing Jelly Babies out of the incision. Using the forceps she holds each of them up to the light to examine them.

All of these Jelly Babies. Peacefully coexisting.

Turnbull But how? How do they manage it?

'Sindhu' Sooner or later, they will all be eaten alive. The trick is to just get on with it.
    Speaking of which.

Turnbull Where are you going? I thought you were going to help me.

'Sindhu' I am, how you say, fucking off back to my country.

Turnbull Wait! Don't go! Oh no. Oh dear.

Turnbull tries once again to reach the packet of Jelly Babies. He tries again. And again. Finally, he succeeds. He picks one out of the packet, squeezes it, brings it to his lips. Unable to bite into it, he panics. Tossing Jelly Babies everywhere.

HELP! I NEED HELP!

Another apparition, 'Young Crea', appears. This is Crea, but it's Crea fifteen years ago, circa 2010. She is glowing.

'Young Crea' Right. How are we getting on?

Turnbull Oh it's you. Thank God. I've had a bit of a wait to see someone real.

'Young Crea' My name is Crea.

Turnbull We met earlier –

'Young Crea' I'm one of the demons that's going to be looking after you.

Turnbull You look younger. Fresher. Radiant.

'Young Crea' It was the optimism.
    This is me fifteen years ago, luv. Newly appointed Deputy Charge Nurse. The NHS was the pride and joy of Britain. Best health care system in the world and I genuinely believed things were only going to get better.

The apparition's voice turns seductive.

Let's cut to the chase. We both know what we're here for. Would you like to have a look?

Turnbull Um. Yes. Yes, I would.

'Young Crea' reveals two healthy cabbages and holds them in front of her chest.

Dear God. Those are some wonderful cabbages.

As Turnbull admires the cabbages, 'Young Crea' takes out a butcher's knife and chops one in half violently. She reaches into the innards of the cabbage and finds a manky, never-ending scroll of paper. She unravels the scroll and hands it to Turnbull.

That's a very large number.

'Young Crea' Your bill, Mr Turnbull.

Turnbull This is outrageous.

'Young Crea' Oh! That'll be an extra six hundred and fifty pounds, I just glanced in your direction.

Turnbull Here. Now. I am the client. I am in control. Patient. I'm the patient.

'Young Crea' Listen here, ya wee prick. You are my marketplace and I am here to suck you dry.

Turnbull Um. I don't think I want that. I am a man, not a marketplace. My body is a temple.

'Young Crea' I'm the highest bidder. I love my job. I really do.

'Young Crea' picks up the metal spike and begins to slather it with lavender oil.

Mmm. Lavender. So invigorating.

She raises the lubricated metal spike as if to launch it up his arse.

Turnbull AAAH! AAAAHhhh!

We see Turnbull burst through the curtain and run into the main space.

3.8

The moon has risen directly over the HOLE *and begins to dapple the space with light.*
The following action may overlap with the end of Scene 3.7, converging on Turnbull bursting through the curtain.
Isla is still seated with Tersia, who repeats the words that are rattling through her mind like some sort of prophecy. Sensing her chance to escape, Isla removes the boots and slowly slips away.

Tersia It all comes falling down and then the endless darkness. Snowfall. Everything white and deathly still. Until. The gloaming at dawn. From the furthest corners most unexpected a heartbeat. Two heartbeats in sync. Then three. Then more. Everything will die and be reborn.

Tersia removes her headphones. Music permeates the space.
Turnbull enters, crashing through his curtain.

Turnbull My body is a temple.

Tersia Shut up and dance with me.

Tersia grabs Turnbull and spins him around the floor. A dance of death.
Ani emerges, pushing Mr Hopper's bed beneath the HOLE. *She stops and applies the brakes. The moon is directly over the* HOLE, *its beams illuminate Mr Hopper's face.*
Mr Hopper gazes in wonder at the night sky. The CURTAIN BILLOWS *but he doesn't care.*

Ani looks around. There are misting nebulisers everywhere, vulnerable patients are roaming, the controlled drugs cupboard is in a total state.
On her way out of the unit, Isla is intercepted by Crea.

Crea There you are.
Where were we?

Crea looks behind Isla and sees the chaos.

Give me one moment.

Tersia casts off Turnbull.
Turnbull drops to his knees.

Turnbull Julie! My Julie.

Tersia walks towards the audience, laughing. She is at the height of her delirium.
She collapses. With skill and synchronicity, Crea and Ani see to reviving Tersia.

Act Four

4.1

Pod B. Four a.m. Turnbull is asleep upright, following his K-hole.
Crea sits next to him, stroking his back. She sees to him with tenderness.

Turnbull Oh. I must have fallen asleep there.

Crea Have some water.

Turnbull Oh that's good.
So thirsty. Thank you. I was in this field of Jelly Babies. Jelly Babies everywhere. All bloated and buoyant. Frosted.
I'm talking rubbish. What a load of rubbish.
And you were there in your. Oh no.
And then, do you know, I thought I'd seen skies opening, and there was a man all laid out, his face was lit by the moon, and I was dancing, twirling around the place with a mysterious woman.

Beat.

Must have been dreaming.

Crea You were given some pretty strong painkillers, Mr Turnbull. By accident.

Turnbull Oh, I asked for them. I was in a tremendous amount of pain. I was quite short with that young nurse.

Crea There has been a significant clinical error, and our department is at fault.

Turnbull I had tried to get the attention of the proper nurse, but she was preoccupied with the man with the moonlit face.

Crea We've had you under observation and run some tests. You should be all right to go home. I've arranged a taxi for you. I'll give you a wee phone about it once you've had a chance to get some rest.

Turnbull Earlier this evening, Charge Nurse Crea, I was a bit short with you as well.

Crea It's all right.

Turnbull No. Let me explain.

Crea You were in pain.

Turnbull My wife. She developed some symptoms during the pandemic – a strange itch, some spots. We waited ages for an appointment. Finally went to her appointment, and she was told it was nothing. Get some creams, they said. Her symptoms worsened. She booked another appointment. And another. Waited. Waited some more. We just did what we were told. We were in and out of here a few times. I should have, um. She went to her third appointment only to be told she had Stage Four liver cancer. We were told it could have been picked up if she'd come in earlier.

Julie. Julie she was called. And I miss her so very much.

Crea Mr Turnbull. I'm so sorry.

Turnbull Well. I must say, overall, you know, this has been a reasonably pleasant experience.

(*Noticing some plaster on his jacket.*) What on earth is all this?

Crea Anytime. Mr Turnbull. Anytime.

NMC PANEL HEARING: SECTION THREE

A shift.
Nursing and Midwifery Council (NMC) Hearing. The linens cupboard transforms into a boardroom, from where the NMC Panel Chair speaks into a desktop microphone. Turnbull remains in the world of the play while addressing the NMC Panel Chair.

NMC Panel Chair The panel should note that a further complaint was received by the department from a Mr Fred Turnbull, with the respect to the night in question.

Turnbull I would like it to be noted and thoroughly considered that although my care was adequate, and the events surrounding my medication error were handled with due candour. I have accumulated a significant dry-cleaning bill due to the plasterwork from the collapsed roof. Please find the relevant documents attached.

4.2

Lina approaches Crea.
The swivel chair is now covered in an orange clinical waste bag.

Lina Nurse Ani said you wanted to see me.

Crea I've seen quite a lot in my day, but ketamine in a nebuliser . . .

Lina I was trying to help.

Crea Under no circumstances are you permitted to administer medication alone. You should know that. Controlled drugs require a two-nurse check. Technically, you're not even one nurse.

Lina You told me to use my initiative.

Crea I told you to work under supervision within the limitations of your skill set.

Lina How am I meant to use my initiative if I'm just stuck observing all the time?

Crea Observation is the most important skill in nursing. The routine observation of patients' vital signs was originally a nursing intervention. Did you know that?

Lina No.

Crea Nursing is the art and science of observing the person directly in front of you. Airway, breathing, circulation. Are they warm, cold, cyanosed, clammy? Are they hydrated, are they oxygenated, are they motivated? Have they eaten? Have they overdosed? Can they afford to feed themselves? Are they in pain? Are they nauseous? When did they last move their bowels? Do they have capacity? Have they been coerced? Can they mobilise? Are they alert, orientated, restless, oedematous? Is the medical care they are receiving in line with their values and desires? Do they have meaningful support in their lives? Has the dog been left alone in the house? How do they take their tea? If you're going to make someone a cup of tea on the worst day of their life, you'd better get it right.

In an age where no one has any attention left to give, it's your job to care.

Lina Well, what about the man in Bed Four then?

Crea What about him?

Lina The nurse just wants him to die with some dignity.

Beat.

Crea You can go home now. I'll be in touch with your uni and they will come back to you in due course.

Lina Am I going to fail this placement?

Crea You have a decent enough bedside manner. Unfortunately, however, you could have killed us all.

Lina If I fail this placement, I won't pass my course. I thought you were desperate for nurses.

Beat.

Not that desperate, clearly. When Nurse Ani left me on the floor, I think I like had a moment, where I like really started to get it. The whole nursing thing.

Crea (*dry*) What's for you won't go by you.

Lina lingers awkwardly.

Lina The young girl with the bruising. I was watching her from the drugs cupboard. She's not okay.

Crea Most patients in the department at this time aren't okay. Do you have anything more specific to add?

Lina No. I just have this feeling.

Crea (*dismissive*) Thanks for your advice.

The HOLE *in the ceiling expands.*

4.3

A rush of new admissions in Pod B. Ani is rushed off her feet. Billy enters, passing through.

Ani Billy! I need your help. I've got five admissions.

Billy What can I do for you?

Ani It's Mr Hopper. Bed Four. He's just about to pass.

Billy . . . What do you want me to do?

Ani Can you just go and sit with him? Just for a few minutes?

Billy Ani.

Ani Please, Billy. I'm run off my feet here.

Billy Right, okay. Five minutes.

Ani Thank you.

Billy Wait, what am I meant to –

Ani is away.

Okay.

Billy goes to sit next to the dying Mr Hopper.

All right. You're all right.

Billy gently takes Mr Hopper's hand to hold.

There we go.

Mr Hopper You came.

Billy Erm.

Mr Hopper Your hands. They're so soft.

Billy Uh. Thanks. There's some Nivea in the break room. Thought I'd give it a bash. Glad it, uh, seems to be working.

Mr Hopper My son. My son.

Billy Uh. It's Billy. But aye sure ye can call me what you like.

Mr Hopper I didn't think you'd come, right enough.
Been a long time since someone has held my hand.

Billy Been a while since I held a hand myself, to be fair.

Mr Hopper One year.

Billy What was that?

Mr Hopper One year Ah've been sober, son.
That's why I've not been in touch. Ah've let you down so many times before and I wasnae gonna do it again. Best wait one year. Then I could be back in contact. I was going to take you camping.

Billy I'll try and pass that on for you, Mr Hopper.

Mr Hopper What did you get up to today, son?

Billy Today? Just, um. Mainly been, er, portering.

Mr Hopper Just nice to hear your voice.
Did you enjoy yourself?

Billy Oh, aye. I do, you know. We never really feature in the medical dramas, us porters. But try doing a heart transplant without someone bringing you a heart.

Can you do one more thing for me, son?

Billy Sure. Ah. What is it?

Mr Hopper Could you just keep talking for me. Your voice is bringing me peace.

Billy I'm a bit out of my depth here.

Mr Hopper Just keep talking, son.

Billy Joke. What's a good joke?

Took a patient to the operating theatre earlier. Turns out he had a change of heart.

Ba-doom-ching!

Righto. Shut up, Billy.

Thirty-odd years I've been telling that joke.

Wheeling folk up and down these corridors. You see some things in here. You hear some things as well, some things can never be unheard. There's grief so great that you think the world should stop turning. But then you turn a corner, and no, the world's just cracking on ahead like it never even happened. You go outside and the world is completely oblivious.

Maybe we've got a bias towards the light. I get that. I do.

It's her kindness that kills me. Just radiates out of her. It's in her bones. Not that strawberries and puppy dogs kind of kindness. There's real muscle to it, you know? Pure strength.

We never got the timing right. She had this and I had that. Then one day she came over to mine, sat on my sofa wearing my trackie bottoms. Babbling on about her day over a bottle of wine. And I've never been the same since.

She's tired. I reckon she's been tired about ten years now. It's crept up on her. The way one glass of wine turns into five. About as much as I want to hold her, I want her to come over, curl up on my sofa and rest.

Mr Hopper stirs.

Shhhh . . . You're all right, Mr Hopper. It's just coming up on five in the morning. Dayshift alarm clocks are about to go off. Cooks, cleaners, physios, auxiliaries. Nurses from Motherwell to Manila. What a project, eh? What an undertaking.

From the ashes of war, they dreamt up a New Jerusalem, a National Health Service. Free at the point of delivery, cradle to grave, so no one should suffer in silence.

Where is the vision today, eh? Look at the state of this place. Slowly bleeding out unchecked. Like a socialist entity in a capitalist system. Parcelled up and fed into a black hole of greed.

I watch the very thing she's best at slowly break her to pieces.

Something really sticks in your throat.

After some time, Billy checks to see if Mr Hopper is still alive.

Mr Hopper I really didn't think you'd come.

Thought I had all the time in the world. You're here now, and that's what matters. You were the only good thing that ever came out of my life. As long as you know that – I can rest.

Billy I'm gonna pass that on for you, okay? I'll find a way to pass that on.

4.4

Crea approaches Ani.

Crea Ani. Can I have a word?

Ani Of course.

Crea I was just reviewing the documentation for Tersia. With her heart rate and temperature, her vital signs were meant to be monitored hourly. She collapsed at 2:45. The last set of numbers you have written down for her is at one in the morning.

Ani I know. I.

Crea Had you caught a change in her vitals she might have been escalated earlier.

Ani She's come to no harm. She's recovering from her UTI.

Crea That's not the point.

Ani I meant to go back but.

Crea But you were clearly preoccupied with the man in Bed Four. Given the pressures on the unit, I'd given you clear instructions to leave him be.

Ani No one should –

Crea I told you no one was to be within one metre of the hole. Let alone a palliative patient. I don't know what you were thinking.

Ani I guess I had a moment.

Crea A moment? You guess you had a moment?

Ani Yeah.

Crea Ani, you've always been a steady pair of hands. But I'm going to raise a concern about your practice.

Ani I had fourteen patients under my care, one one-to-one, one palliative and a walking catastrophe of a student.

Crea Staffing levels will be considered. We both have a duty of candour here. This isn't a punishment. It is an opportunity to formally reflect on our practice.

Ani You know what, I'm done. I'll be handing in my notice.

Crea Ani.

Ani Don't worry, I'll stay until the end of my shift. You'll need your numbers.

Billy, from Mr Hopper's bedspace, waves Ani over.

Billy Ani! I think it's time.

Ani Excuse me.

Ani crosses over to Mr Hopper's bedspace. Crea exits.

4.5

Mr Hopper's bedspace.
  Mr Hopper's last moments. An impromptu ceremony.
  Ani and Billy hold Mr Hopper's hand. Silence, or Ani might sing.

Ani Goodbye, Mr Hopper.

Billy Bye, pal.

Perhaps a rope ladder descends from the HOLE, *and Mr Hopper climbs it, waving goodbye.*

Ani I'll get the doctor to pronounce it.

Silence.

Some shift.

Billy You're telling me.

Ani Thanks for your help, Billy.

Billy No bother, hen.

Ani That was a nice note to end on.

Billy Don't get carried away now. Still a few hours left in the shift.

Ani I'm done with nursing.

Billy What are you on about?

Ani Crea was going to raise a concern about my practice. I just decided to hand in my notice.

Billy Based on tonight?

Ani Guess I went a bit rogue.

Billy Crea's losing the plot. She's hardly left this place. You're a nurse to your bones, Ani. You're a brilliant nurse.

Ani You think so?

Billy Of course I do.

Ani I don't know. I've been thinking about it for a while now. I saw this advert, the other day. They were looking for people to clean swimming pools in Alicante. Now I've got this fantasy of driving around in a wee purple four-by-four, tunes blaring, a bunch of tools strapped to my roof. Doing something completely different.

Billy Well on ye go, girl. Spread your wings. You'll fly.

Ani sees to Mr Hopper's body.
  Billy spots Crea at the staff base.
  He sanitises his hands and heads over.

4.6

Crea is bed managing. She moves colourful squares across a large monitor. It's high-stakes Tetris. Billy approaches.

Billy Everything okay?

Crea More or less.

Billy Ani mentioned you were going to file a concern about her practice.

Crea I don't know what's gotten into her. She's handed in her notice.

Billy She's one of your best nurses.

Crea We have been haemorrhaging staff across the board.

Billy I know you've always run a tight ship, Crea. But is that not an argument for cutting some slack?

Crea The service is under a lot of pressure. I need to be able to rely on my staff.

Billy The service needs to be able to retain staff.

Crea And someone needs to keep this place functioning to a reasonable standard.

Billy The girl's father died alone in hospital.

Crea (*taken aback*) Well I didn't know that, did I?

Billy It's like trees in a gale. The ones that survive bend in the wind. Those that are too rigid are ripped out, roots and all.

Crea You're going to tell me how to do my job?

Billy What do I know, right? I'm just a porter.

Crea Oh and I meant to say. I can't do Saturday. With Ani's resignation it would be all temporary staff in here, this place would be a riot. It wouldn't be fair to anyone. Maybe some other time.

4.7

Crea goes over to see Isla.

Crea I had a look at your notes. You were in here a couple of times a year ago with deliberate self-harm.

Isla Yeah.

Crea Have you been getting any help?

Isla Everyone does their best.

Crea I've spoken to medical staff and someone from our psych team is going to come down and see you. Would that be okay?

Isla Yeah. Whatever.

Crea I just wanted to, um.

Isla You wanted to try and convince me that my life is worth living. But you're needing to do it in two minutes or less.

Crea . . .

Isla It's okay. I get it. You're busy.

Crea This walk you went on.

A low rumble from the collapsing roof.
  Crea notes it in her peripheral vision but tries to retain her focus on Isla.

Isla I don't want to talk about it.

Crea How are you feeling now?

Isla I'm fine. I'm actually feeling a lot clearer.

A loud crack.
  The ceiling gives way.

Crea Hold that thought. Can I get a hand here?

All staff rush in to tend to the collapsed roof.

Act Five

5.1

One hour later. Parts of the collapsed roof have been tidied to one side and cordoned off.
Mr Hopper is now in a white body bag. Billy wheels him down to the morgue.
Meanwhile, Ani helps Tersia drink a cup of tea.

Tersia Where am I?

Ani You're in hospital, Tersia. You took unwell with a wee infection.

Tersia I can't remember a thing. I was at the flat, I'd just come back having gone out to get some milk, and I just cannae remember.

Ani That's probably the delirium.

Tersia Look at this. It's the weather forecast from the paper. Scattered snowfall overnight. Gibberish scrawled all over it. That's my handwriting. I was tuned to the moon. And I don't know why I have these boots. Haven't worn these in years. Must have dug them out.

Ani What is it you normally do?

Tersia I'm a lollipop lady. Keep myself to myself. I can remember shouting. Oh, I hope I wasn't too much bother. I'd be absolutely mortified if I gave you any bother.

Ani You were no bother at all, Tersia. You were an absolute dream of a patient.

Tersia I bet you say that to all the girls.

Ani I'm glad you're on the mend.

Tersia You make a great cup of tea. That was perfect.

Ani Ta.

Tersia And nurse? Thank you. For taking such good care of me.

Ani It was my pleasure.

5.2A

Crea is surveying the damage from the collapsed roof. Ani and Billy are working nearby.

Crea Have you managed to get a break, Ani?

Ani Yes. You look like you could use a break as well.

Unit Phone You are number thirty-seven in the queue.

Billy How's the roof looking?

Crea Safe to say it's fucked.

   Beat.

(*To Billy.*) I'm sorry.

Billy You're all right.

Crea Do you want to come eat chocolates with me in the linen closet?

Billy Yes. Yes, I do.

Crea I am going to take ten minutes, Ani.

Ani Sure. No bother.

Billy and Crea head to the linens cupboard, slink down and sit on the floor with a box of chocolates. She puts her head in his lap.
   Ani sees to Tersia.

5.2B

Lina returns to the unit. She wears an overcoat over her nursing uniform.

She takes the keys to the drugs cupboard from her pocket. She glances in the linens cupboard and sees Billy and Crea sharing a moment. She looks around for someone else to give the keys to.

NMC PANEL HEARING: SECTION FOUR

A shift.

Nursing and Midwifery Council (NMC) Hearing. Lina remains in the world of the play while addressing the NMC Panel Chair.

NMC Panel Chair Are you chewing gum?

Lina It helps with my anxiety. Can I just say? I don't think you understand what nursing school was like. One minute you're at uni and it's all like essays and multiple-choice questions and the next minute you're just chucked out into the wild and people are asking you questions and expecting you to do things. To be honest with you, it's a bit of a shock to the system.

NMC Panel Chair If we could focus on the issue of the keys.

Lina There was a red key and there was a green key. The staff nurse had said don't touch the red key, but I mixed them up. Which in my defence, like what if I was colour-blind?

NMC Panel Chair Are you colour-blind?

Lina No.

NMC Panel Chair Our concern is not with the colour of the keys, but where they were left on your departure.

Lina Well I accidentally took them away with me.

Beat.

But I brought them back.

NMC Panel Chair And what did you do with the keys when you returned to the unit?

Lina Well I tried to give them to someone, but the Charge Nurse was busy.

NMC Panel Chair Busy doing what?

Lina I don't know, she was like hanging about in the closet eating chocolates with the porter.
So I just left them.

We fade back into the unit.
  Lina drops the keys on the main counter and leaves.

5.2C

Scenes 5.2c and 5.2d can be played with some overlap.

Billy Nice to see you taking your break for once.

Crea The way this night has panned out I'm going to be here till dayshift lunchtime writing incident reports.

Billy You'll need a few of these to keep you going.

Crea This place.

Billy The thing is, Crea. You've got to put it all in context –

Crea Oh, don't start with the politics, Billy? Who has time for all that?
Lately all my dreams are of this place. And they're all the same.
I hear this banging. I go to the front entrance of the hospital, and I see this sea of people.

And it's all those people that were banging their pots and pans during the pandemic. But this time they're angry. I can hear them shouting.

I freeze. I'm scared that they are angry at us – all these people in corridors, discharged too early, all the missed diagnoses.

But then a woman calls out to me and beckons me to join. And I get swept right up in the crowd and I can see that they're going somewhere. Not the direction everything is headed but somewhere else, to a place where people care about each other. Its electric, the clamour, and I'm shaking my keys, cos it's all I've got on me. Keys. My keys.

Crea sits up and bolts out.

5.2D

Meanwhile: Ani finishes helping Tersia drink a cup of tea. Ani goes to leave, Tersia calls her back.

Tersia Nurse! Nurse!

Ani What can I do for you?

Tersia Can you do me a favour?

Ani Anything.

Tersia Could you give these boots to the young girl?

Ani The girl.

*Dread. Ani knows. She looks for Isla.
She checks her pocket for the controlled drugs keys.*

5.3

The controlled drugs cupboard has been ransacked by Isla.
   Isla is in the patients' toilet cubicle.
   Code. Crea and Ani attempt to batter down the door, joined by Billy and other members of staff.

NMC PANEL HEARING: SECTION FIVE

A shift.
   Nursing and Midwifery Council (NMC) Hearing. The linens cupboard transforms into a boardroom, from where the NMC Panel Chair speaks into a desktop microphone. Crea remains in the world of the play while addressing the NMC Panel Chair.

NMC Panel Chair Crea Harrower. The panel has concluded that the only sanction that would adequately serve the public interest is a striking-off order, effective immediately.

Crea I would like to state for the record that my career as a nurse has brought me a tremendous amount of fulfilment. It has been the privilege of my life to serve people.
   If there's one thing I've learned from years of being in charge. Someone needs to have a plan. A clear vision of how the night is going to pan out, the values and standards that will be maintained, whether or not the roof is caving in.
   What is the plan here? Because you can see the direction everything is headed. All this loneliness and isolation. What is the vision?
   I still believe in the principle of this service. Where care is delivered based on medical need and no other criteria. A place where no one suffers in silence, and everyone is seen.
   But somewhere in all of this, someone must be accountable.
   As for the loss of that beautiful young life, *I have only myself to blame.*

The door opens. Isla is dead, having overdosed in the patients' toilet on controlled drugs.
  We might see the figure of Isla, wearing Tersia's beautiful boots ascend into the night sky.

EPILOGUE

Eight months later. The HOLE *is covered over with a tarp.*
  The linens cupboard. Billy is sat inside with a coffee. Senior Charge Nurse Ani enters, looking for him. She wears crisp navy blue.

Ani I thought I'd find you in here.

Billy You're back!

  Beat.

I still like to take my breaks in here from time to time. Old habits die hard.

Ani How is she?

Billy She's okay. Made it out to the garden yesterday. Planted some lavender.
  Look at you. Crisp navy blue. She'll be so proud.

Ani Do you think?

Billy Of course. I thought you'd moved to Alicante. Couldn't hack the sunshine?

Ani I had a change of heart. It was the day I went to her hearing.

Billy Spread your wings. You'll fly.

Ani Best get to it then. Onwards and upwards.

  The End.